The Journey Before Us

Critical Issues in American Education

Lisa Michele Nunn, Series Editor

Taking advantage of sociology's position as a leader in the social scientific study of education, this series is home to new empirical and applied bodies of work that combine social analysis, cultural critique, and historical perspectives across disciplinary lines and the usual methodological boundaries. Books in the series aim for topical and theoretical breadth. Anchored in sociological analysis, Critical Issues in American Education features carefully crafted empirical work that takes up the most pressing educational issues of our time, including federal education policy, gender and racial disparities in student achievement, access to higher education, labor market outcomes, teacher quality, and decision making within institutions.

Judson G. Everitt, *Lesson Plans: The Institutional Demands of Becoming a Teacher*

Megan M. Holland, *Divergent Paths to College: Race, Class, and Inequality in High Schools*

Laura Nichols, *The Journey Before Us: First-Generation Pathways from Middle School to College*

Daisy Verduzco Reyes, *Learning to Be Latino: How Colleges Shape Identity Politics*

The Journey Before Us

First-Generation Pathways from Middle School to College

LAURA NICHOLS

Rutgers University Press

New Brunswick, Camden, and Newark, New Jersey, and London

Library of Congress Cataloging-in-Publication Data

Names: Nichols, Laura, author.
Title: The journey before us: first-generation pathways from middle school
    to college / Laura Nichols.
Description: New Brunswick: Rutgers University Press, [2020] |
    Series: Critical issues in American education | Includes bibliographical
    references and index.
Identifiers: LCCN 2019009122 | ISBN 9781978805620 (pbk.: alk. paper) |
    ISBN 9781978805637 (cloth: alk. paper)
Subjects: LCSH: First-generation college students—United States. |
    Minorities—Education (Higher)—United States. | People with social
    disabilities—Education (Higher)—United States. | College preparation
    programs—United States. | Student aspirations—United States.
Classification: LCC LC4069.6 .N54 2020 | DDC 378.1/98—dc23
LC record available at https://lccn.loc.gov/2019009122

A British Cataloging-in-Publication record for this book is available from the British Library.

♾ The paper used in this publication meets the requirements of the American National
Standard for Information Sciences—Permanence of Paper for Printed Library Materials,
ANSI Z39.48-1992.

www.rutgersuniversitypress.org

Manufactured in the United States of America

For Niamh and the futures of all children

Contents

The Journey Before Us

Introduction

"Trying to Do School"

> School plays a big role in our own dreams and ambitions because school in itself is trying to sell you this dream of you can do anything you want and you should go to college to be able to live up to this expectation. Of course, there's the expectations that one has to meet these expectations, that are put on you by someone else, and you don't really ever fully understand what you're really getting yourself into.
> —Samuel

Samuel walked into Saint Middle School his first day of sixth grade with nervous anticipation.[1] He was excited to attend Saint, a small school in his neighborhood designed for students with academic potential whose parents are immigrants, have a very low income, and have experienced little formal education in their home countries, but want the best educations for their children. Shy at first, Samuel loved school and learning new things. After being pushed to excel at Saint, Samuel received a full scholarship to one of the area's most competitive private high schools, where he participated in sports and clubs from the start of his first year. But the transition to high school was bumpy, his grades started to fall, and he became unsure of himself. Five years after graduating from high school Samuel says he is "going to college. Well, trying to do school." He has already attended one for-profit four-year school, the local state college, and two community colleges. He works, often the overnight shift, and takes classes during the day. He loves science and is hoping for a degree in engineering. But he is avoiding taking chemistry, a class that has vexed him at every school. Excited about a STEM club meeting he recently attended at his community college, Samuel feels like he is on a good path but is frustrated that it is so difficult to navigate going to college and getting a degree.

Samuel's experiences capture the historical role and promise of education in the United States. His middle school, like his elementary school, promoted the ideal of going to college to "break the cycle of poverty through education." And across the United States the idea that every student who works hard can go to college, what Tressie Cottom (2017) refers to as the "education gospel," permeates our school systems. Millions of members of previous generations attest to this ideal. The education gospel is particularly salient in immigrant communities, as children aim to fulfill the dreams of their immigrant parents who left what they knew to start the journey for increased opportunities, especially for their children. But college degrees, promoted as the ticket to financial well-being, have now become attainable mainly by those who already started out in the highest social classes (Alexander, Entwisle, and Olson 2014; Bjorklund-Young 2016).

The Problem: Low College Completion

In the past there was concern that students and parents did not fully understand the need for training beyond high school, that the problem was cultural. But today students are expected to attend college, and this has increased the academic effort of students in high school across all social classes (Domina, Conley, and Farkas 2011; Kalogrides 2009). Further, these beliefs have been translated into behavior via college enrollment. Yet rates of college completion are dismal and in some cases getting worse, particularly for students from low-income and even middle-income families. While over 60 percent of students from high-income families receive a bachelor's degree eight years after high school graduation, only 15 percent of those from the lowest income families do (Cahalan et al. 2016). This is despite similar rates of postsecondary enrollment and intention for college completion.

We are facing what some have termed a "completion crises" in postsecondary education (Itzkowitz 2018). And for an increasing number of students, college enrollment has actually made their lives worse, leaving them with no degree and debt (Carnevale and Smith 2018; Liebenthal 2018; Miller 2018).

At the same time, most well-paying occupations require at least a bachelor's degree, and thus education can still be a path to economic mobility. Low-income students who get into the most prestigious colleges typically graduate and can even move from the lowest to the highest social class by the time they are thirty, in the same generation (Chetty et al. 2017). But few students who would benefit the most from attending selective schools with plentiful student supports and high graduation rates even apply (Hoxby and Avery 2013).

The positive impact of going to college is not just for individuals and their families; there are also societal implications. It is estimated that over 65 percent of future jobs in the United States will require training beyond a high school degree (Carnevale, Smith, and Strohl 2014). In California alone, if bachelor's degree graduates increase only at the current pace, by 2030 the state will need to find over a million additional workers to meet the demand (Johnson, Mejia, and Bohn 2017). As college has become necessary for a greater proportion of people in the United States, spaces at colleges have not grown at a similar rate, and schools cannot accommodate all students who aspire to go to college. Further, the cost to attend private *and* public colleges has far outpaced inflation, and financial aid has not kept up.

Most K–12 students are similar to Samuel in that their parents do not have college degrees. Only 33 percent of children in the United States live in households that would be considered continuing-generation college (CGC), where at least one parent has a bachelor's or graduate degree.[2] To overcome the college completion crisis, we need more students whose parents did not go to college to obtain degrees. However, first-generation college (FGC) students are actually a *shrinking* proportion of our college population (Cataldi, Bennett, and Chen 2018; Saenz et al. 2007).

Because of data showing the immense inequity in college completion by social class, a number of initiatives are being proposed to try to improve college outcomes by challenging states to take greater responsibility for educating low-income students. For example, the American Talent Initiative has a goal of enrolling fifty thousand high-achieving students with significant financial needs to colleges with high graduation rates by partnering with selective public and private schools that pledge to increase their enrollments of low-income students (Anderson 2017), and Promise Programs across the United States aim to provide free or near-free tuition at state schools (Miller-Adams 2015). But to accomplish such goals, educators and colleges must understand the situations of the students they are trying to enroll and make sure that necessary supports are available through the full application, enrollment, and completion process, especially as students transition through the many phases of becoming and being a college student. To truly address the completion crisis, we need to understand the educational paths of a greater number of potential first-generation and low-income students (Beattie 2018; Rondini, Richards, and Simon 2018).

The majority of studies on college completion by educational background start with students already in college or graduating high school. But doing so misses many students like Samuel who are in and out of different types of colleges or who never enroll. *The Journey Before Us* follows students who would be the first in their families to attend college while they are in middle school. The students all attended Saint Middle, a school for sixth- to eighth-graders from low-income families that was designed to prepare students for rigorous academic work, get them into high schools that send their graduates to college, and stay with students through their full educational trajectory. Saint is part of a network of independent nonprofit U.S. middle schools that are locally formed, strategically placed in low-income neighborhoods, privately funded, and designed to serve middle schoolers from low-income families with no or underperforming schools in their communities.

As a sociologist who has spent many years in and working with a number of nonprofits in the neighborhood where Saint is located, I had always heard about the school but knew little about it. Most recently I learned from parents at the local public elementary school about their strong desire for their children to be accepted to Saint, seen as a "golden ticket" to educational success and a path to better high schools and ultimately college. Acceptance to the school was a starting point that parents believed made their own difficult journey north from Mexico and other parts of Latin America, with little education and money, worth it because of the opportunities it opened up for their children. To understand Saint's approach to education and its potential lessons for the larger education system in the United States, I spent a year observing the graduate support program, interviewing fifty-one alumni, and analyzing the trajectories of all of their students since their first class graduated in 2004.

In the process of following students' educational journeys from middle school to young adulthood, I examine the paths that students take as they transition to different types and levels of schools and what factors help and hinder their progress. Focusing on students at Saint provides an opportunity to learn from students who can test the myth that in the United States, regardless of family background, hard work and success in the education system can lead to social mobility.

By learning from the experiences of students who are academically prepared and who desire to be the first in their family to attend college and following them through the U.S. education system, we can better understand what contributes to completion and where things fall apart for students on their path to a postsecondary degree. And we can use this information to consider more fully how we as a country want to respond to and fix the fissures in the U.S. education system.

The College-Going "Path"

Going to college is often described as a path that students take—a path that already exists, that has been taken by others; all students need to do to get on that path is to work hard and follow directions and they will arrive at the same destination as everyone else. The few books and growing articles about FGC students often include in their titles references to colleges paths, such as "Clearing the Path" or "Breaking a Path" or "Being on the Path." But what is that path exactly, and how does a student get on it?

What it *really* takes to be and stay on the path to a college degree is often hidden. Many prospective FGC students do everything that students whose parents have college degrees do, including expecting to attend college from an early age, working hard in school, getting good grades, being involved in activities and motivated for school, meeting all the college application deadlines, and so forth. But what first-generation students usually do not see are the ways that upper-class parents are hoarding extra advantages for their children (Calarco 2018; Lewis and Diamond 2015; Lewis-McCoy 2014) and how high schools that upper-class students usually attend are structured to allow their students to "sparkle," providing a good cultural match to quality colleges (Nunn 2014). As a transitional generation, aspiring FGC students differ from CGC students in that they also have to learn, usually with little help and at an early age, how to get and stay on the college path, including explaining the process to family members, getting over feeling different from the those whose families have "always gone to college," figuring out how to pay for college and living expenses as well as help with family needs, and navigating important decisions in college such as choosing a major and knowing the right courses to take.

The traditional path to college, that is, enrolling in the best college a student is admitted to, attending full-time right after high school graduation, and living away from home, is an ideal that results in the greatest chance for timely degree attainment. But the traditional path to college for students assumes a number of things: (1) that students are exposed to quality K–12 education systems; (2) that they have people easily accessible when they need help, whether it be tutors or counselors or parents or family members; (3) that students have grown up in safe neighborhoods and are surrounded by neighbors, coaches, parents, and friends who have attended college as well as opportunities to participate in extracurricular activities; (4) that students do not need to help their families financially while in school; and (5) that the schools they attend will have high success rates of degree attainment and ample support to transition students to the next phase of their desired schooling.

An increasing number of programs have been developed to get more FGC students on the traditional college path. The strategy has often been focused on helping FGC students mimic the college-going behaviors of CGC students. While these strategies have helped a few more students go to college, they have been insufficient to graduate large numbers of students. Further, a focus on individual programs does not provide an opportunity to problematize potential faulty assumptions behind the "college for all" promise (Nathan 2017).

First-generation students are likely to assume it is their fault if they struggle more than students whose parents have college degrees, not realizing that the path is set up for those whose families have resources that allow them to devote their time and attention to being a student, do not need or require them to continue to help at home, and can graduate with little or no debt. These conditions are true for only a small proportion of children growing up in the United States today (Ziskin et al. 2010).

The Focus of This Book

There are many researchers who study college completion and the college experiences of students who come from low-income families. *The Journey Before Us* extends this work by taking a longer view of students' trajectories and focusing on the importance of transitions. First, we see what it takes for those who are part of transitional generations, as first-generation college students, to attempt social mobility via education. Seeing the paths that aspiring first-generation college students take and adapt to meet their goals illuminates what needs to change for more students to complete a bachelor's degree. Learning from those in transitional generations illuminates the larger policy and societal realities in which we live. Second, we see that the transitions between schools (from elementary to middle school, from middle to high school, and from high school to college) are crucial times for students on the path to a college degree.

What this book shows is how the design of the ideal college path as well as the invisibility of the larger journey to get to college works against the success of FGC students, for whom getting to and staying on the path is a long process through many different schools, neighborhood conditions, and barriers contrary to staying in school. In looking at students' trajectories, with a sample of students linked to their middle school, we can see what happens to them over time, through multiple school transitions and experiences, giving us a clearer view of what it takes to obtain a college degree when you are a FGC student.

The conclusions in this book are based on the direct experiences of students. After attending public elementary schools and Saint Middle, students then enrolled in a variety of high schools, including private, traditional public, and charter schools, resulting in five different paths post–high school: (1) the traditional path of college enrollment away from home, (2) a hybrid approach of enrolling at a four-year school while still living with family, (3) a working student path that combined full-time work and attendance at a two-year college, (4) a meandering path like Samuel took with enrollment in many different types of postsecondary institutions with lots of dead-ends, (5) and a work/family route that included working and taking care of family members without being in school.

The factors influencing why students were on certain paths as well as what they needed within and across paths will guide the suggestions in later chapters for improving college pathways for potential FGC students. The student experiences give important clues about what needs to change to improve the educational journeys of young people and the societal effort necessary to address the college completion crisis. This book cannot or does not speak for all first-generation college students; however, the students profiled here and the analysis that follows aims to help readers, from any educational background, understand what it takes to be a member of a transitional generation and to consider that the journey before us is one that must be collectively embraced if education is to once again be a force for social mobility.

While the main focus of *The Journey Before Us* is the experiences of students, analyses of national data are also included to offer a fuller understanding of patterns on a larger scale. Further, the students profiled in this book allow for a simultaneous consideration of our own educational journeys and how the individuals we were linked to, the schools we attended, the neighborhoods where we lived, and the policies that existed supported or challenged our ability to stay on our chosen path. In the process of this examination, specific information for students, schools, and policy makers is revealed that can be used to structure our educational trajectories in ways that open up pathways to better address the needs of transitional generations.

1

Paths Diverged

─────────────────────────●

Student Outcomes by College Generational Status

> My parents didn't go to college. I have no idea what it's like, I have no idea academically what it's going to be like. And then there is a bunch of other kids whose parents did go to college, they've been preparing for it for their whole lives.
>
> —Gloria

It is December of Sarah's senior year of high school and she has just finished submitting her eleven college applications, crossing her fingers that she will be admitted to most of them and know better which one she wants to attend when she has to decide in the spring. Now she can go back to enjoying her senior year of high school. Isabel, a classmate of Sarah's, has seen the flyers and emails from school counselors about college workshops and visits but has not had time to attend most of them. Besides her schoolwork, she is working at the local amusement park, helping her single mother paint houses on the weekends, driving her younger siblings to school, and completing her required school volunteer hours to keep her private high school tuition low. As Isabel is the oldest child, her mom, sister, and brothers are very excited about her being the first in her family to graduate high school in the United States. When asked what she will do once she graduates, she says that she wants to go to college. But she knows it will be expensive and that her mom relies on her to help with her siblings as well as keep her business going.

Sarah and Isabel are both seniors and attend the same college-prep high school, St. Theresa Catholic, where most of the students graduate in four years and attend college as full-time students the following fall. But Sarah and Isabel came to St. Theresa via two different routes. And although they had access to the same resources at their high school, had similar grade point averages, and, with the support of their families, had desired to attend college since they were children, their paths to and within college are very different, with Sarah having a high likelihood of obtaining a bachelor's degree in four years and Isabel much less likely to graduate, even in six years. Why?

To increase rates of college graduation, we need to understand how current college-going paths support some students and not others. The purpose of this book is to show, through the experiences of students and young adults who are the first in their families to navigate the U.S. education system, the paths they take starting in middle school and the resources they need to transition their families from first-generation to families with college backgrounds.

To do this we will learn from the educational journeys of students who all attended Saint Middle School and aspired to attend college. Each chapter begins by outlining the experience of one Saint alum—Samuel, Isabel, Alex, Veronica, or Ali—and adds further detail from the experiences of other Saint alum. Chapter 2 includes information about what is known already about schools and educational success based on the educational background of parents. Chapter 3 covers the experiences of Saint alumni in middle and high school. Chapter 4 shows the different paths that Saint alumni took post–high school. Each of the paths has something to teach us about what needs to improve if a greater number of aspiring students who want to be the first in their families to attend college are to realize their goals. Chapters 5 and 6 discuss the main themes revealed in the experiences of students over their educational trajectories and what can be done to improve the experiences and outcomes of prospective first-generation college students.

All of the students profiled in this book started at public elementary schools in a low-income urban neighborhood in California, then attended Saint, a private, Catholic middle school designed to provide educational options for low-income, mostly second-generation immigrant students in the United States, then moved on to a mix of traditional public, charter, and private high schools, and finally followed one of five different paths post–high school. Their experiences, both when they were prospective college students in middle and high school and later as they attempted to attend college, show the importance of understanding that moving through the education system in the United States is a journey that needs to accommodate many different pathways. Further, by focusing on transitions we can see what changes are necessary so more students graduate.

There were five factors that high-achieving students who would be the first in their families to attend college needed to enroll and ultimately graduate with a bachelor's degree: (1) actively being put on the path to college early on one's educational trajectory and receiving certification and recertification of belonging on the path by schools at every transitional stage; (2) access and opportunities to attend quality schools and colleges with good rates of graduating students; (3) assistance from trusted individuals with the know-how to navigate the different systems that students encounter on the path to college, especially when transitioning to different schools; (4) economically stable families, and (5) the ability to balance work and school.

The rest of this chapter provides background information on the growing importance of degree attainment in the United States and what is known about the influence of parents' educational background on students' educational trajectories. These areas are explored using an ecological systems approach to understand the full context of students' lives and how their journeys are intertwined with their families, schools, neighborhoods, and social policies.

The Growth and Stagnation of Educational Attainment in the United States

The educational backgrounds of adults in the United States have risen over time, and rates of high school graduation are increasing. As we can see in figure 1.1, in 1940 only 20 percent of the adult population had a high school degree, but now the rate is close to 60 percent. And the proportion of adults

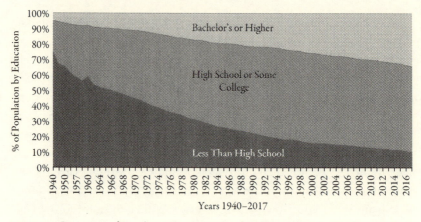

FIGURE 1.1. Percentage of Population Twenty-Five and Older by Education Level, 1940–2017. Data and figure design from U.S. Census Bureau, 2018.

with a bachelor's degree is also growing, although at a slower pace. However, some of that increase is the result of immigration policies that have led to the recruitment of already educated adults to join the U.S. workforce. For most adults in the United States, their highest level of education is high school or less (National Center for Education Statistics [NCES] 2018a, 2019).[1] But the necessity of postsecondary training for jobs of the future, especially in tight labor markets, is growing, with a particular need for those with bachelor's degrees (Carnevale and Smith 2018).

This book shows that the meritocratic system of education and hard work, which propelled many baby boomers (parents and grandparents of current young adults) into the middle class, is not working in the same ways because structures of opportunity have changed. It also chronicles the slow progression of inequality that has existed for families with few economic resources for many generations but is now also negatively influencing those in the middle class. Paradoxically, those same parents and grandparents who worked hard and were the first in their families to attend college between the 1960s and the 1990s are the ones hoarding the very uneven educational resources that exist for children in the educational pipeline today.

Millennials, those born between 1980 and 2000, are the first generation to be worse off economically than their parents at the same age (Taylor 2014). And income inequality between the generations is vastly different. In 1984 those sixty-five and older had ten times the net worth of those under thirty-five; by 2011 that difference was twenty-six times. This despite the overall higher levels of education of young adults compared to their parents and

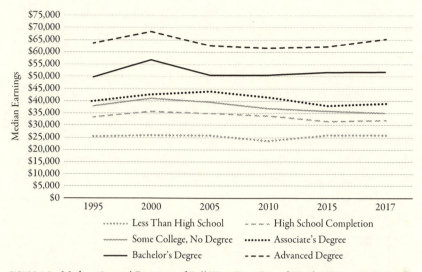

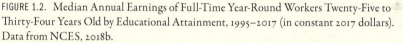

FIGURE 1.2. Median Annual Earnings of Full-Time Year-Round Workers Twenty-Five to Thirty-Four Years Old by Educational Attainment, 1995–2017 (in constant 2017 dollars). Data from NCES, 2018b.

grandparents. These differences between the generations have policy implications. The largest voting bloc in the United States, baby boomers, grew up at a time of great expansion of both public and private educational institutions as well as public financial support for college, even during the Great Depression of the 1930s (Mettler 2014). Those who benefitted from these increasing opportunities often see only their hard work as explanations for their success. Hard work is still extremely necessary, but there also must be opportunities to put that hard work toward something that is a valued good in society. Traditionally that opportunity has been found in education, and many generations of adults in the United States, including those from immigrant families, have found social mobility in one or two generations via hard work and success in the education system.

Some argue that attainment of a bachelor's degree is not necessary for everyone. But with the increasing credentialization of our society, and as figure 1.2 shows, earnings of those with bachelor's or graduate degrees have consistently been higher than wages for those with only some college. Earnings with an associate's degree, usually a two-year degree, are only marginally better than those with a high school degree. Postsecondary education, especially a bachelor's degree, is now necessary to attain a middle-class lifestyle, and more jobs are requiring such credentials (Carnevale and Strohl 2010). This means that a collaborative effort is needed between state and federal government, higher education, and the private sector to figure out how to ensure that more students whose parents do not have a college degree go to college. These aspiring first-generation college students are the focus of this book.

First-Generation College Students

Although there is some disagreement about how first-generation college (FGC) should be defined (Beattie 2018), in this book FGC students are those who plan to enroll or have enrolled in postsecondary education and whose parents' highest degree is high school or less. Continuing-generation college (CGC) students are those who have at least one parent who has a bachelor's or graduate degree.

At the same time that an increasing number of adults in the United States have a bachelor's degree or higher, the proportion of students in four-year colleges who are also the first in their families to attend college is decreasing. According to data from the Cooperative Institutional Research Program's (CIRP) Freshman Survey, the proportion of students at four-year institutions who are FGC has fallen. In 1971, 38.5 percent of first-time, full-time college students were FGC, compared to just 15.9 percent in 2005 (Saenz et al. 2007). In 2016, 19 percent of college students identified as FGC (Eagan et al. 2017). But the proportion varies widely by college. In a survey sent to all second-year students at five California public university system campuses, 34 percent of the sample was FGC or had parents with some college experience (Vuong, Brown-Welty, and Tracz 2010), while at a comprehensive public university in the Midwest, 58 percent of the sample was FGC (Ishitani 2006). These percentages typically do not include the large numbers of FGC who go part-time and/or attend schools other than four-year bachelor's-degree-granting postsecondary institutions.

Differential Paths to College Degree Attainment

Let us return to Sarah and Isabel. They both know that attending college, especially attaining a bachelor's degree, is good for their future. Their parents are supportive and encouraging. They have worked hard and performed equally well in school. Why then are their experiences so different? Why did they end up at different points in that critical time during their senior year of high school? Figure 1.3 gives some clues. The chart is based on analysis of data from a national study that followed the same students from high school until

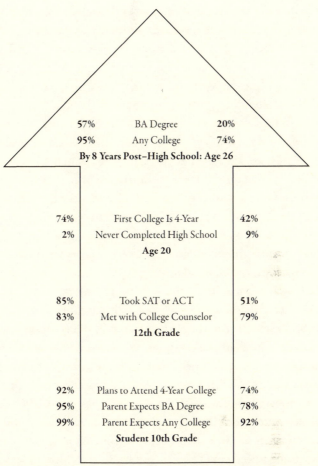

FIGURE 1.3. Comparing First- and Continuing-Generation Students, Tenth Grade to Age Twenty-Six. Data from NCES, 2017, Education Longitudinal Study, 2002/2012.

age twenty-six. Comparing outcomes based on the educational background of students' parents, interesting similarities and differences are evident.

In tenth grade both groups of parents want their children to attend college and students expect to as well. However, a smaller percentage of parents who have a high school degree or less expect their high schoolers to attend a four-year college compared to parents who have a college degree. And while both groups of students have similar rates of talking to a college counselor by twelfth grade, a much smaller proportion of the first-generation students had taken the ACT or SAT, usually necessary to apply to four-year colleges. As time goes on, the differences between the two groups begin to get even greater: 74 percent of the continuing-generation students attend a four-year college as their first college, while only 42 percent of FGC students do. That is Isabel. And because there are very low rates of transfer from two-year to four-year schools, even among very talented and motivated students like Isabel, her likelihood of achieving a bachelor's degree has decreased significantly by attending a two-year school first.

As a result, while both FGC and CGC students have high rates of attending college by the age of twenty-six, relatively few had earned a bachelor's degree eight years after their 2004 graduation from high school. Of CGC students, 57 percent had done so, compared to only 20 percent of FGC students. In comparison, 68 percent of CGC students who were twelfth graders in 1992 had received a bachelor's degree eight years after high school graduation, versus 24 percent of FGC students (Chen and Carroll 2005). Students in both groups are now less likely to complete a bachelor's degree within eight years of high school graduation.[2]

Looking at changes in the social mobility patterns of immigrants is one way to understand these trends. Free public education has been part of the opportunity structure in the United States for many immigrants and their children for more than two centuries. White European ethnic groups in the late 1800s and early 1900s benefited from the growth of U.S. mass education, which allowed Irish, German, Italian, and other immigrants (Sarah's great-grandparents) to witness the social mobility of their children in just one or two generations (Keister 2007). But that is not happening for many new immigrants today. Even students considered to be part of the middle class are being priced out of higher education, left with debt not experienced by their parents. Further, it usually takes students six or more years to achieve a bachelor's degree at the more affordable public colleges (Gordon 2018; Rivas-Drake and Mooney 2008).

The Path to College: Educational Journeys by Parental Education

Students from Saint understood that their educational aspirations were part of a longer journey to continue the hopes and dreams of their immigrant parents and also to put their future children on a better path. But this is an unknown journey. Said one Saint alumnus, "I'm the first one to ever go to college in my family, so I didn't know what the journey was, what the process looks like."

Analyses that look only at the individual efforts of students or the combined efforts of parents and students are limited in that they do not consider the full context and educational trajectories of students. Research has shown that the schools that students attend and the neighborhoods where they grow up are significant in predicting educational outcomes (Johnson, Mejia, and Bohn 2017; Owens 2010; Sampson 2012), especially as students become adolescents and move into young adulthood (Alvarado 2016). Parents with educational backgrounds can also provide a "smoothing" effect, helping their children as they transition to different schools and ensuring that they have everything they need to keep them on the college path.

The reason why college-going is reproduced in families and why students born into families where their parents graduated from college are also likely to graduate is the result of being born onto a "path of least resistance" to college. For students born onto the college path, maintaining the path is easier than falling off; it is a journey that is shared and reinforced by family, friends, community, and the larger society. As Tressie McMillan Cottom (2017, 65) says in *Lower Ed*, "You have to work hard *not* to go to college." Pressure and support come from many areas that make staying on the college path an unquestioned activity. The system itself is also set up so that students able to take the "traditional" path to college are more likely to reach their destinations.

Today social class sets the educational paths and outcomes of students. Social class influences the neighborhood where one lives and the resources that are there, including access to adults with requisite degrees as well as the quality of the public schools that one attends (Goyette 2014). A combination of factors sets students on a path of least resistance to college, where almost all of the influences they encounter support graduating from college.

What the experiences of students profiled in this book highlight is that for students not born onto the college path, they must exert immense effort to get on and stay on the path. Students need tremendous support for that journey. And structures need to change. College used to be more affordable than it is today. Entry-level jobs allowed college students to work and cover the cost of tuition and obtain a degree in a reasonable time frame. Yet the cost of college has risen dramatically faster than have entry-level wages, and the most affordable schools typically serve large numbers of students and graduate a small proportion. To produce a larger number of adults with bachelor's degrees in the United States, we must figure out how to make the college path more open and less dependent on individual good luck.

By looking at the paths of students who are the first in their families to go through the U.S. education system and would be the first in their families to go to college, the challenges they face on the paths that currently exist, and the larger journey that involves family, culture, schools, work, and policies, we can better understand and address issues faced by FGC students. Seeing how what students need shows up as "social desire paths" (Nichols 2014) on the way to college points to necessary solutions. By focusing specifically on what Saint Middle School did to get students and keep them on the college path, as well as when that broke down, we will be able to better describe how college-going paths need to change and evolve.

Understanding Students' Educational Journeys in Context

In this book the ecological theory of human development is used to guide the analysis of the wider social context in which children live and where schools, communities, and policies operate (Bronfenbrenner 1979). This theory influenced the Head Start preschool program in the mid-1960s, formed to address the negative effects of poverty on children. The approach includes four different system levels: the micro level of students and their families, the meso or organizational level of schools and programs, the exo or neighborhood level, and the macro level that consists of social policies and the larger societal context.

Characteristics of Aspiring First-Generation College Students

As in the past, FGC students are often disproportionately represented by students whose families have low incomes and belong to ethnically or racially underrepresented groups as well as are new immigrants to the United States. As table 1.1 shows, more than a quarter of FGC students who attempt education post–high school in the United States are Latina/o. In the fall of 2016, of college students who identified as Latina/o 57 percent were FGC (Eagan et al. 2017). Students of Latina/o descent are the fastest growing group of FGC students.[3] By contrast, a high proportion of CGC students are white (70 percent).

Going back to Sarah and Isabel from the beginning of this chapter, Sarah is white and her family came to the United States and began their educa-

Table 1.1

Generational Status of High School Sophomores Who Enrolled in Postsecondary Education by Race/Ethnicity: National Sample of U.S. Students

	First-Generation College Students (%)	Continuing-Generation College Students (%)
White/European American	49	70
Black or African American	14	11
Hispanic or Latina/o	27	9
Asian/Asian American	5	6
Other race/ethnicity	5	4

SOURCE: Table reformatted from Redford and Hoyer (2017); based on analysis of the National Education Longitudinal Study of 2002 about students who had any postsecondary experience.

tional journeys multiple generations ago. As a result, her grandparents and parents are all college graduates, which allowed them to acquire professional-level jobs that paid wages of the upper class, and they began to acquire wealth in the form of home ownership, college savings, and investment accounts, all means to finance her private education from the very beginning of her life. Sarah can go to the college of her choice or the "best" college she gets into because her family has the economic resources to pay the tuition and living expenses and can afford for Sarah to be out of the labor market while she attends college.

Although families from Mexico have been migrating to the United States for many generations, Isabel's family is part of a more recent cohort of immigrants who were recruited to work in the low-wage job market in the 1990s (Selee 2018; Stephen 2007). Her parents had little access to formal education in Mexico and few opportunities for social mobility, hence their migration north. Isabel is the first generation in her family to have attended formal schooling full-time in the United States.

Table 1.1 reflects what we would expect given the history of immigration patterns to the United States. White European Americans began migrating to the United States in large numbers in the 1700s and 1800s. As North America developed as a country, education became more formalized. Mass migration from Europe coincided with the development and growth of K–12 schools and colleges, including financial aid for college. This allowed the children of European immigrants to take advantage of the growing education system, and education thus became a force for social mobility. As a result of this history, many CGC students have parents, grandparents, and even great-grandparents who obtained a postsecondary education in the United States.

In contrast, indigenous people from what is now Mexico have not been able to benefit from the early development and investment in the U.S. education system. Further, many labor agreements have propelled workers from Mexico and Latin America to come to the United States for low-wage work (Ngai 2004). In the past the work was primarily agricultural and required workers to move with the harvests. Any children who came with their parents moved around often and could not sustain their enrollment in school. However, today's labor market for low-wage immigrants requires less mobility, allowing children to stay in the same schools over time, resulting in more students continuing their education (Gonzales 2016). As a result, like the European immigrants of the past, today's children whose parents migrated from Latin America, currently the largest immigrant group in the western U.S., have increasing rates of high school completion and college enrollment.

In 2016, the largest proportion of high school graduates who were Latina/o enrolled in college (at 47 percent), similar to the share of white high school graduates who enrolled (Gramlich 2017). Over 3.6 million Latinas/os were enrolled in public and private colleges in the United States; however, college completion has been extremely low compared to that of other groups. Currently Latinas/os have the lowest share of twenty-five- to twenty-nine-year-olds with a bachelor's degree (15 percent compared to 41 percent of European Americans, 63 percent of Asian Americans, 22 percent of African Americans) (Pew Research Center 2016). Like the European immigrants of the late 1800s and early 1900s, Latinas/os are growing group of students in the United States seeking social mobility via education (Pew Research Center 2016).

FGC students are also much more likely than their CGC counterparts to grow up in families living in poverty. In California 48 percent of adults with less than a high school degree are poor, including 26 percent of Latinas/os. Latinas/os have the highest poverty rate of any race/ethnicity that is measured using the California Poverty Measure (Wimer et al. 2018).[4]

Almost all (95 percent) Latinas/os in California under age eighteen were born in the United States (Education Trust–West 2017), and Latinas/os are 51 percent of those under age twenty in California. Currently 55 percent of all students in California's K–12 public school system identify as Latina/o. Given this background, and since the start of Saint Middle School in 2001, almost all Saint students have been of Latina/o heritage. This is because Saint was created to serve the neighborhood, traditionally a community for new immigrants—Italians in the early 1900s and immigrants from Mexico and other parts of Latin America today. Most of the alumni from Saint are second-generation immigrants (born in the United States to parents born in Latin America) and live in families where their parents have less than a high school degree and are economically below or near the poverty line.

Family and Structural Influences

At the individual level, the economic resources of the family children are born into have increasingly been the most important factor in predicting educational outcomes. Compared to their CGC peers, a larger percentage of FGC students come from lower income households: that is, those that make $20,000 or less (27 percent vs. 6 percent) and $20,001 to $50,000 (50 percent vs. 23 percent). Conversely, a lower percentage of FGC students come from households in the three highest income categories (Redford and Hoyer 2017). This is not surprising given that education, occupation, and income are so closely linked to one another, with those in the highest paying occupations typically having at least a bachelor's degree.

What has changed though is the necessity to have connections via parents, what sociologists refer to as social capital, to help with smoothing the entrance into college as well as finishing college and finding internships as well as employment. As Laura Hamilton notes in *Parenting to a Degree*, "Educational and professional success almost requires moderate to extensive financial, emotional, and logistical parental support through college and the transition to the labor force" (2016, 3). Given these current realities, how are FGC students to be on equal footing with students who have a cadre of support and people pulling them through college (Nichols and Islas 2016)?

The other difference for this generation of college-goers is the extremely high cost of college. We will talk about this more when we discuss how social policies have changed and how many students are now required to take out loans and receive less aid compared to previous generations. And so the family one is born into, especially the combination of the educational background of parents, the economic resources of the family, and immigration status (whether immigration happened long ago or recently and if that migration was chosen or forced) combined with social conditions are important factors in understanding college completion.

Organizational Brokering: Saint Middle School

At three o'clock the bell rings in the two-story building that houses Saint Middle School. Lockers slam shut as students stow their books, but only for an hour. Although classes are officially over, the school day is not. After a short activity period, students move into structured homework time, where they receive tutoring from teachers, local high school students, and volunteers. Once a month they also attend Saturday school, which includes academic work, college visits, and enrichment field trips. And in the summer students take six weeks of language arts and math classes at a local private high school. The Nativity school model, on which Saint Middle is based, provides structured supports for students born into neighborhoods and families with few economic resources and offers students the ability to compete with their peers already on the path to college by middle school.

Nativity middle schools operate throughout the United States as private nonprofit schools designed to provide quality educational options for very low-income students who live in neighborhoods with no or very low-quality middle school options. For a typical graduating class at Saint, 50 to 70 percent gain admittance to the most competitive college-prep high schools in the community. Alumni of Nativity schools have a high likelihood of enrolling in college (Nativity Miguel Coalition [NMC] 2018). However, as we shall learn from the students profiled in this book, this path can be personally painful and these interventions are not always enough to firmly move low-income students who would be the first in their families to graduate high school and college in the United States to a stable path and a college degree.

Saint is located on the property of a church that is also full of activity, providing food and other resources to community members during the week and offering religious services, mainly in Spanish, on the weekends. At a time of waning participation in formal religious activities in the United States (Galen 2014), services here are full. Attendees at Saint Church mainly live in the neighborhood. The school, Saint Middle, was started as an initiative of a former minster at the church. Members of the church, including the current pastor, serve on Saint's board, and the church and local Catholic private college provide a full-tuition scholarship for one student from the neighborhood each year. Often these recipients have attended Saint Middle.

About 10 percent of all K–12 students attend private schools, of which approximately 36 percent are Catholic (NCES 2018a). Many private schools were started by religious organizations, sometimes to counter perceived discrimination in public and private schools or to teach religious beliefs within the school curriculum. For example, Catholic schools in the eastern United States grew in response to early discrimination against Catholics, particularly in the higher education system. As such, new immigrants as well as early settlers had access to free, quality Catholic education. In the western United States, where my interviews took place, religious colleges were some of the first to be formed (Goodchild et al. 2014). Schools such as Saint play particularly important roles in the lives of new immigrant families as religious organizations continue to be active contributors to the socialization of new immigrants in the United States.

Neighborhood Factors

Most of the houses in the neighborhood where Saint students live were built in the early 1900s when the community was an enclave for newly arrived immigrants, mainly from Italy. Small apartment buildings and partitioned houses provide the bulk of housing for families who mostly rent.

After attending Saint Middle School, which Isabel could easily walk to from her family's apartment, she traveled each weekday to her high school, St. Theresa, less than five miles from Saint, but in Sarah's neighborhood. As we can see in table 1.2, the neighborhoods are very different.

Where Sarah is growing up there are fewer children and most people are in their forties or fifties and own their own homes, the median household income is over $150,000, only 5 percent of residents live in poverty, and 75 percent of residents have a bachelor's or graduate degree. In contrast, in Isabel's neighborhood the median income is much lower, it has more residents as families live together to afford rent, and a much smaller proportion have completed college. About 23 percent of families live in poverty based on the national poverty line of $25,100 for a family of four. This is an underestimate of the percentage of families who have a difficult time making ends meet, as Isabel and Sarah live in a city where the cost of living is among the highest in the United States.[5]

By living in a neighborhood where most of the residents own their own homes, have college degrees, and work at jobs that pay a middle-class or higher wage, Sarah has an advantage over Isabel who grew up around adults who have not gone to college, do not have wealth in the form of home ownership, and are barely able to make their monthly costs. Individuals, families, and schools live and operate in neighborhoods. While students and families move,

Table 1.2
Comparing Isabel and Sarah's Neighborhoods

	Isabel's Neighborhood and Saint Middle School	Sarah's Neighborhood and St. Theresa High School
Median age of residents	29	44
Median annual household income of residents ($)	39,780	150,642
Married couples where both parents work (%)	85	79
Residents 25+ with a bachelor's degree or higher (%)	11	75
Families in poverty (%)	23	5
Residents in owner-occupied homes (%)	19	83
Residents per square mile	16,984	6,899

SOURCE: Data from American Fact Finder by census tract (2016, https://factfinder.census.gov/faces /nav/jsf/pages/index.xhtml) and city-data.com.

most stay in their current locations and attend neighborhood schools. But when students continue to live in their same low-income neighborhood but attend a school in another community, the change can be jarring. Saint alumnus Suzanne explained it this way: "It's crazy how you are in the same high school, but yet you're coming from completely different sides of the world."

Policy and College Completion

The institutionalization of mass public K–12 education in the United States has slowly applied to policies related to postsecondary education as well. A combination of public and private funds supported the very first colleges formed in the United States (all private). Then the federal government, along with the states, began to set aside land specifically for institutions of higher learning. The Northwest Ordinance of 1787 stated that "religion, morality, and knowledge, being necessary to good government and the happiness of mankind, schools and the means of education shall forever be encouraged" (as quoted in Mettler 2014, 114). Institutions beyond high school proliferated at a high rate, especially in the West. Enrollment rose quickly, the result of low tuition.

The GI Bill after World War II spurred enrollment even further. The numbers of college-goers doubled on some campuses in the years between 1943 and 1946 and increased most noticeably among men from families with limited incomes (Thelin 2004). Tuition actually declined relative to family income in the 1940s and 1950s, and "the baby boom generation came of age during this period, making for more Americans who were college ready than ever before" (Mettler 2014, 119). The Pell Grant program started in the early 1970s and provided further support for students with limited means to pay for college. However, as college tuition has increased, Pell Grants have paid for a smaller and smaller proportion of the cost of attending public colleges. During the 1976–1977 school year, federal Pell Grants covered almost 80 percent of the average undergraduate tuition, fees, room, and board for public four-year colleges (Center on Budget and Policy Priorities 2017). In 2016–2017 less than 30 percent of costs to attend the same public colleges were covered by the maximum Pell Grant. As a result, rapidly rising tuitions have made even public four-year colleges out of the financial reach of low- and middle-income families.

And so the higher education landscape that is available to Sarah and Isabel is very different from that of the past when there was wide public and private support for higher education and policies that assisted students in college who did well in the meritocratic system of education but whose families did not have economic means. Changing structural realities have meant that today the greatest predictor of success in education is the economic status of the family students are born into. Students from low-income families might even do worse financially if they attempt to attend college, accruing large sums of debt and potentially not being able to finish with a degree that would allow them to obtain a job where they can repay that debt (Miller 2018). This is the current situation we find ourselves in and why FGC students in particular face structural constraints to obtaining a higher education. Further, other factors important to those transitioning to adulthood (Settersten 2005, 2011) and outside of students' educational experiences, such as work, a family's economic stability, and federal policies targeting vulnerable populations, influence future FGC students' ability to stay in school and on the path toward a college degree.

Besides learning more about Isabel and Samuel, in the chapters that follow we will also meet Alex, Veronica, and Ali as well as a number of other first-generation students. Their experiences demonstrate the effects of school transitions and the particular issues that first-generation students face on the path from middle school to a college degree. These students are our best barometers of whether it is true that the United States is still the "land of opportunity" it was once known to be and what transitional generations can teach us about how we can revive this ideal.

2

Being a Transitional Generation and Navigating Schools

──────────────────●

> Being first generation to go to college, we have the hardest part. Our parents had to get us here, to raise us, that's hard. But then we have to go through many years of school and find a job on our own. We have to set up a stable environment to bring up our own kids so finally, they can have more of a diverse path that they can take; so they can do what they want, all because I've set up a stable environment for that.
> —Alex

Alex always knew that he would go to college and where. His mom, who raised him on her own working two jobs, always told him, "Your only job is to go to school." Although he did not like the long school days, Alex did well at Saint, making friends easily and excelling academically. He earned a full scholarship to a private high school, where "there was a lot of wealth." His scholarship allowed him to play football and hockey because it covered all the equipment and fees, barriers to participating before high school. But Alex's transition from Saint to high school was difficult: "All the students from Saint felt out of place, we stuck to our little group and then some of us eventually branched off and made other friends." When it came to applying to college, his counselor encouraged him to apply to highly ranked University of California (UC) campuses and private colleges. He did, mainly to appease his counselor, but he paid the acceptances no attention: "I always planned to go to Local State U because it's close to home and cheap and I could live with my mom."

Schools and Opportunity

As we saw from the data in chapter 1, students aspire to go to college and their parents support them. However, inadequacies in public K–12 schools by social class have resulted in students who are born into low-income families and would be the first in their family to attend college often falling off the college track. Further, even if students go to quality schools and stay on the path to a college degree, the structure of college has not changed to meet the increased demand. The disconnect between what the culture values and promotes and possibilities in the current structure of our society is referred to as a structural lag: culturally the belief in attending college has permeated our society and is a desired good, but structurally colleges have not adjusted to the large numbers and different circumstances of most students seeking a degree.

When there is structural lag in organizations and they do not meet the needs and goals of those with the desire to engage in such organizations, people do the best that they can to get current structures to work for them. For first-generation college (FGC) students who struggle to or cannot take the traditional path to college, how they adapt these structures to meet their needs and accomplish their goals can teach us a lot about how our educational systems and colleges need to change if we want to make postsecondary education more accessible and college degrees more achievable for a greater proportion of students.

To better understand the students in this book, this chapter provides the theoretical foundation to situate FGC students as members of a transitional generation. The concept of transitions is located in the literature and understood from the experiences of students' educational trajectories from middle through postsecondary school as it relates to being a potential FGC student and a child of immigrants transitioning to adulthood. The students profiled in this book all started at public elementary schools in a low-income neighborhood, then attended Saint Middle School, which was designed to provide educational options for low-income, mostly second-generation immigrant students, then moved on to a mix of traditional public, charter, and private high schools, and finally transitioned to five different paths post–high school. Their experiences and insights can instruct schools to change in ways that would benefit all aspiring college students.

After laying out the case for considering FGC students as members of a transitional generation, data are presented to look more deeply at the role of private and public schools in the educational trajectories of low-income, first-generation students. The role of Catholic schools, which historically have served as cultural brokers for new immigrants acculturating to the United States and also provided a large network of schools to promote the social mobility of Catholic immigrants, is reviewed. Beyond outcomes, the chapter includes insight into how resource availability during students' transitions influences why students are making the choices they are and provides further insight into how schools and policies need to change so members of transitional generations will have a better chance of finishing college. The chapter concludes with more information about the students and schools profiled in this book.

Transitional Generations

Alex, Isabel, Samuel, and the other students we will meet in *The Journey Before Us* are all FGC students, first in their families to be on the path to a college degree. As such, they have navigated transitions in ways and sought resources that many students whose parents have gone to college take for granted. Transitional students can teach us a lot about the factors, mechanisms, and components necessary to help more students successfully complete their degrees. Students' experiences also give us a sense of the larger journey that students are on, a journey that started with their parents and has implications for their own future children as well as later generations.

Taking an even larger view, seeing what FGC students grapple with can also be instructive for those who are the first in their families to try other types of new experiences. This can include being the first in one's family to travel abroad, pursue an occupation never tried before, go away to college, date outside one's race, and so forth. These new experiences can be exciting at the same time that they also involve facing unknown realities and finding new forms of support. Those who are the first in their families to pursue a goal must figure out, often on their own, how to transition from one normative path to another. This usually requires an ability to straddle different cultural and structural worlds, including different values, norms, lifestyles, jobs, pastimes, and rules.

The concept of "transitions" has been most widely explored by psychologists as experiences that individuals go through and the subsequent strategies counselors can use to assist individuals facing any number of transitions such as losing and finding a job, changing relationship status, becoming an "empty nester," or transitioning to different roles (from childless to parent, etc.) (Langenkamp 2011). Not surprisingly, this research has focused on the individual level and the coping resources that are necessary to get through a transitional period. Schlossberg, Waters, and Goodman (1995) advise counselors helping clients going through transitions to focus on four Ss: situation, self, support, and strategies.

The students interviewed for this project allow us to expand our knowledge of transitions. First and foremost, we explore what students need to transition to being the first in their families to attend college. Further, the students profiled in this book are also a transitional generation in that most are the children of immigrants and are often a bridge between their parents' home country and the United States. Finally, we consider not only students' educational trajectory from middle to high school and then on to postsecondary experiences but also their transition to adulthood. The students in this book are experiencing all of these transitions. Their stories help us understand how a societal institution, such as the U.S. education system, can be structured to better accommodate the journeys of aspiring FGC students. This is necessary if we want to address low college graduation rates.

Before looking into these transitions, we must also understand the idea of generations as used in this book. Demographers usually use the term generation to refer to cohorts of individuals who are born in the same period of time, such as Generation X, the Millennial Generation, and others. In talking about students who are first- or second-generation college students or first- or second-generation immigrants, the idea of generation is used in relation to the status of individuals compared to their parents. In this case generation is tied not to the year of their birth but rather to family and in particular to how parents' background affects their children.

Generation matters when considering educational outcomes.[1] Students who are third-generation college attendees, where both grandparent(s) and parent(s) have college degrees, are the most likely to attend the most selective colleges and to receive the most help with college planning as well as resources from their parents when applying to schools (Lawrence 2016).[2]

The experience of being a transitional generation is the result of not only being born a part of a particular generation but also being a member of an intergenerational family, as Alex notes in discussing the connection between his mother, himself, and his future children. Because families' lives are intertwined with each other, across generations, we know that these "linked lives" impact one another (Elder 1985; Marshall and Mueller 2003). In this book we explore the experience of being part of a transitional generation as a process that occurs within families, organizations, neighborhoods, and larger societal contexts.

First-Generation College Students as a Transitional Generation

Defining college students by parents' educational background is a relatively new phenomenon. In the 1950s researchers began to focus on the experiences of students in college based on their social class status. The development of the term "first-generation college" was influenced by the passage of the GI Bill, which increased the college-going rates of students from low-income families, fundamentally changing the demographics of colleges (Walpole 2003, 2007). Adachi (1979) is credited with promoting the idea of "first generation" college, which was used to determine eligibility for federal TRIO programs (Pitre and Pitre 2009). TRIO defines a first-generation college student as one for whom neither parent (or one's primary parent) completed a bachelor's degree. Adachi claimed that income was not enough to determine eligibility for TRIO programs, but rather that students should be both low income *and* first generation (Billson and Terry 1982), signaling an acknowledgment that being FGC was more than economic and included potential cultural factors such as family knowledge, expectations, and values.

Researchers are finding that parents' educational background has grown more influential than social class, especially in predicting a student's likelihood of applying to a selective college (Turley, Santos, and Ceja 2007). Studies thus now define FGC students as an identifiable group beyond social class, with some researchers emphasizing that being first generation is a structural identity, while others focus on FGC as influenced more by culture than by structure (Beattie 2018).[3]

The earliest research found that FGC students often feel like they are moving between two different cultures and worlds (London 1989; Lubrano 2005). Without parents to help them navigate the college process, students sense that they are alone in the process. And although their parents are supportive and want to help them, students usually have to make important decisions about their schooling without fully understanding the landscape and implications. For example, Mari, whom I interviewed for this project, did not learn what Advanced Placement (AP) courses were until the end of her junior year of high school, when she attended a meeting about applying for college and an advisor presented on how to manage AP credits. "I was very angry at [my high school]. No one explained that to us and when I asked about it, they were like, 'You didn't know?' And I said, 'How am I supposed to know?'" By then it was too late for her to enroll in such classes. And at college Suzanne did not realize that by only taking twelve units per semester, as required by her financial aid, she would never graduate from her private college in four years. This delayed her graduation and cost her additional tuition. Without background and experience and parents who understand how school systems work, FGC students do not even realize what questions they should be asking.

Researchers who privilege culture in their analyses of the experiences of FGC students have argued that FGC students do not have the same knowledge of the cultural context of college that helps continuing-generation college (CGC) students succeed. FGC students often feel disconnected in college and can be confused by the required separation between family ideals and knowledge versus what is valued and expected in the higher education context (London 1989; Pérez and McDonough 2008). These cultural factors impact how FGC students experience college (Kim and Sax 2009; Pike and Kuh 2005; Terenzini et al. 1996). In one of the few studies with FGC students who dropped out of a four-year selective university in southwestern Ontario, many students said that they had trouble "fitting in" and "feeling university" and were not able to "relate to these people" (Lehmann 2007, 105). These feelings of disconnection and lack of integration at the university ultimately contributed to students dropping out and seeking educational and professional opportunities at community colleges and through apprenticeships. We will similarly see that first-generation students profiled in this book who attended private high schools also experienced very similar feelings of disconnection that threatened their ability to stay at their high schools, even though they knew such schools were their best chance to get into college.

Most of the research on first-generation students has been about their experiences in college, and usually at selective universities (Beattie 2018). However, most FGC students attend less selective colleges and are less likely to graduate when they do (Ishitani 2006; Pascarella et al. 2004). FGC students also tend to have less interaction with faculty compared to CGC students (Jack and Irwin 2018), struggle to understand faculty expectations (Collier and Morgan 2008; Kim and Sax 2009), and have less knowledge of how to act in elite contexts such as private schools (Dumais and Ward 2010; Jack 2019; Lareau 2015).

Of course being FGC is also highly correlated with other individual factors that affect college outcomes such as income, race, and gender. Being born into a family with a high income is associated with higher rates of persistence and likelihood of graduating (NCES 2018a). Being from a racial/ethnic group that is underrepresented on campuses predicts a reduced likelihood of graduating with a bachelor's degree (Dumais and Ward 2010; Ishitani 2006). Being male decreases the likelihood of graduation but does not affect persistence (Ishitani 2006). Apart from college generation status, income, and race/ethnicity, precollege traits such as high school GPA and other academic measures such as SAT scores and the intensity of high school coursework are also included in studies of FGC student outcomes. College GPA (Chen and Carroll 2005 for graduation but not persistence), full-time attendance (Chen and Carroll 2005; Dumais and Ward 2010), and continuous enrollment (Chen and Carroll 2005; Dumais and Ward 2010; Ishitani 2006) are also important predictors of college outcomes for FGC in studies that include those variables in their analyses.

Parental help and school support with college applications, generally considered social and cultural capital variables, are positively associated with college graduation (Dumais and Ward 2010; Pascarella et al. 2004). Researchers who study the role of parents in the college experiences of more privileged students find that parental involvement is necessary in helping students navigate and get the most out of what colleges offer and to move into jobs after graduation (Hamilton, Roksa, and Nielsen 2018). The involvement or not of parents can result in an "effectively maintained inequality" that disadvantages students whose parents have less college experience. Hamilton and colleagues note that colleges, perhaps unintentionally, encourage and at some level expect parents to be involved in the decision making of college students.

Hamilton (2016, 185–186) argues that schools need to understand how they perpetuate and advantage students with college backgrounds and make sure to provide a legitimate "mobility pathway" for all students, something that does not exist in many colleges: "A mobility pathway levels the playing field for students who lack family advantages. It offers long-term and emergency financial aid, ideally in the form of grants, for those who need it. It is built around majors that do not require family interventions to meet the requirements or secure jobs after college." Hamilton is pointing to the growing call that colleges do more to ensure an increasing proportion of FGC students get a fair shot at finishing college. It is also important to remember that regardless of background, families are a major source of support for students, especially families that help their children prioritize education throughout their full educational trajectories (Gofen 2009; Kiyama and Harper 2018).

Income, rising tuition, and reduced government grants are factors that influence college completion; another is the type of institution in which FGC students tend to enroll. Selective private nonprofit colleges have the highest rates of graduation of students with a bachelor's degree in six years (Ginder, Kelly-Reid, and Mann 2017; NCES 2018a). Yet over three-quarters of FGC students attend public colleges, mainly two-year schools, and only 6 percent attend highly selective four-year colleges with high rates of four-year graduation (Redford and Hoyer 2017). There are access and geographic reasons that help explain why FGC and CGC usually attend different types of schools. These reasons will be explored more in the following chapters.

Thus, FGC students as a transitional generation embody both structural factors such as coming from families with low economic status and having gone to low-performing secondary schools, as well as cultural realities such as not attending the most selective schools they can get into and not following the norm of living or working on campus. Because FGC students inhabit these intersecting structural and cultural realities, they can be considered "strategic research material" (Merton 1987) in that they provide a unique opportunity to understand a variety of factors and processes at once and point to key factors that influence postsecondary outcomes.

Children of Immigrants as a Transitional Generation

The term "transitional generation" has also been used to describe the children of immigrants and the distinct role that children play in helping new immigrant families transition to their new cultural context (Zhou 2001). Zhou and Lee (2007, 190) argue that focusing on the experience of the children of immigrants provides an opportunity to determine if mobility and notions of the American Dream are still possible: "As with so many ideological controversies, the issue of immigrant incorporation may be beside the point, as it hinges on the foreign-born, a transitional generation caught between their countries of origin and their new host society. A more fruitful barometer of immigrant incorporation would be the mobility patterns among the later generations, that is, the 1.5 and second generations (i.e., those raised or born in the United States of immigrant parentage). Are the adult children of immigrants moving beyond the socioeconomic status (SES) of their parents, and, no less important, are they advancing to the point where they are on par with native-born Americans?"

The students profiled in this book would be classified as being second-generation immigrants (born in the United States to immigrant parents) and a few are members of the 1.5 generation (born outside but mainly raised in the United States). Alex, who started this chapter, is a second-generation immigrant. He demonstrates what it is like to be a member of a transitional generation. While both he and his mom have similar dreams for him in terms of education, they differ somewhat in how they think about what it takes to be on the college-going path. Alex's mom prays daily before an altar she set up in their apartment. The altar includes the small statue of a saint that represents education. Said Alex, "I don't know what saint it is, but she would pray to it and she would always ask me, 'Why aren't you praying?' And I would always say, 'What's that going to do? I have to put in my own effort and work and whatever I do ultimately is the result of my own work and effort.'" Alex's mom, like many parents of Saint students, believes strongly in the power of hard work and religion; while Alex prioritizes and puts his faith only in the American ideals of work and effort.

Being children of immigrants, especially when their parents do not speak the language of the dominant culture and might not yet fully understand the society to which they immigrated, can put immense pressure on children: "Children of immigrants who tend to become fluent in the host society's language more quickly than their parents and use their language skills to translate, interpret, and mediate between their family and English-speakers, are known as language brokers. These youth do not just translate words; they are mediating between cultures and worldviews, often between their parents and members of the dominate groups and/or authority figures" (Yoo and Kim 2014, 29). Being a translator for parents has been found to have both positive and negative effects on children.

Organizations as Resources for New Immigrants. While immigrant and second-generation immigrant children can provide an individual bridge from parents to others, at the meso or organizational level schools and religious organizations have historically been the main formal socializing entities as families transition to their new culture (McGuinness 1995; Yoo and Kim 2014). Family is representative of immigrants' home country, "while school represents American culture" (Paat 2013, 959). First- and second-generation immigrants need to feel comfortable as they interact with formal organizations in their new culture.

In the next chapter we will see how Saint students felt when they transitioned from attending elementary school and their middle school, where most of the other students were Latina/o and also children of immigrants, to schools where most of the student body was European American and did not understand immigrant communities. This influenced their sense of belonging and caused them to question their ability to perform well. A sense of belonging is important for students' successful transition to college, especially for students who feel that their ethnic identity is underrepresented on campus (Hurtado and Carter 1997). Latina/o students also experience racism and tensions around race and ethnicity at college, which affect their academic well-being (Hurtado 1992; Nora and Cabrera 1996). Thus, the enduring effects of being an immigrant as well as race/ethnicity are important factors in students transitioning to the college-going path.

Being part of the immigrant generation also matters in terms of educational outcomes. In 2004, 58 percent of first-generation immigrants from Mexico to the United States had less than a high school degree. That same year, only 17 percent of the second generation (U.S.-born children of immigrant parents) had less than a high school degree (Waldinger and Reichl 2006). Children born of immigrant parents have some of the highest educational aspirations of any immigrant generation. Yet, once children reach the third generation, their likelihood of succeeding academically is similar to that of later-generation U.S.-born children (Duong et al. 2016). And if these students are raised in poverty, their educational outcomes are generally low.

Children of new immigrants realize the sacrifices of their parents and are often motivated to work hard for the sake of their families. However, researchers who look at intergenerational mobility between different ethnic groups find that children of Mexican parents tend to do worse than other ethnic groups mainly because they are the most likely to attend low-quality schools in poor U.S. neighborhoods (Hao and Pong 2008). As Hao and Pong state, "Downward mobility among second-generation Mexicans may not be reversed without major policy efforts" (2008, 87). In California, with a large proportion of Latina/o students, this issue cannot be ignored if the state is to address its growing shortfall of college-educated workers (Public Policy Institute of California [PPIC] 2018).

Catholic Schools and New Immigrants to the United States. Historically, religious organizations have provided resources to new immigrant communities in ways that ultimately influenced the development of state and federal policies.[4] For example, in New York City, Catholic organizations provided services that ultimately became institutionalized at the state level and then influenced the development of the American welfare state (Brown and McKeown 1997). New immigrants often do not trust governmental organizations, so religious organizations have historically been intermediaries between new immigrants and public resources (Hagan 2012). This is true even today. For example, fearing that those living in the largely immigrant community where Saint is located would be less likely to report crimes and work with the police, the police chief talked at all the Spanish masses at Saint Church to assure residents that the local police department would not report any undocumented residents to Immigration and Customs Enforcement (ICE).[5] Religious organizations are seen as important conduits to immigrant communities.

Combining religion with education has also helped new immigrants gain social mobility in their new culture. In the past Catholic K–12 schools provided opportunities for and addressed educational discrimination against new immigrant Catholics from Ireland, Italy, Poland, and other European countries. Now these schools mainly serve wealthy families. Some current Catholic educators and researchers bemoan the loss of schools for low-income immigrant students today and ask that Catholic schools revisit their original missions and purpose (Higareda et al. 2011; Huchting et al. 2014; Ospino and Weitzel-O'Neill 2016).

Catholic schools, along with Protestant schools, began in the United States in colonial times as moral enterprises (Bryk, Lee, and Holland 1993). Seminaries, free primary schools, and secondary schools were created to recruit priests and later to provide educational opportunities to the growing number of Catholic immigrants from Europe. Until 1825 Catholic schools in New York received public aid and no distinction was made between public and private schools. This approach to funding schools continued in many states, including in rural areas where Catholic schools were sometimes the only educational option for children. Later, as public schools were developed, Catholics interpreted them as Protestant in character and content (Justice and Macleod 2016). Catholic schools then had a mandate to establish "alternative institutions where both their faith and their culture would be valued" (Justice and Macleod 2016, 25). However, new immigrants wanted to acculturate to North American culture and the schools needed to prove their "Americanism." And so "while Catholic schools consciously sought to preserve Catholic values and ethnic identities, they also facilitated the assimilation of immigrants into American public life" (Justice and Macleod 2016, 27). In the early 1900s Catholic schools started to promote themselves as levers of social mobility, and indeed they became such a force.

According to the National Catholic Educational Association, in the 1950s there were over thirteen thousand Catholic elementary and secondary schools in the United States. But by 2015 there were half as many (Ospino and Weitzel-O'Neill 2016). At the height of Catholic education in the United States, 55 percent of Catholics attended Catholic schools at some point in their K–12 educations. Many of these schools were free (thanks to the availability of low-paid teachers who were from Catholic religious orders). The prevalence of affordable, quality Catholic schools in the United States is one factor that likely explains the upward mobility of white Catholics during the 1980s and 1990s that was not experienced by low-income whites as a whole or among those from other religions (Keister 2007).

But things are different for new immigrant Catholics today. While the number of Catholics in the United States has grown from 48.5 million in 1965 to almost 68 million today (Center for Applied Research in the Apostolate [CARA] 2016), most Catholic schoolchildren attend urban public schools and not Catholic schools. And the demographics of Catholics in the United States have changed dramatically from the mid-twentieth century. Today 40 percent of Catholics identify as Latina/o and 60 percent of Catholics under age eighteen are Latina/o, with 90 percent born in the United States (Bureau of Labor Statistics 2013). That is over eight million Catholic school-aged children who are Latina/o (Ospino and Weitzel-O'Neill 2016). However, the proportion of Catholics who attend a Catholic K–12 school is small: only 2.3 percent of Catholic Latina/o youth attend a K–12 Catholic school.

As in the past, many Catholics in the United States are also first- or second-generation immigrants. Of new immigrants, 39 percent are Catholic, compared to 18 percent of U.S.-born adults (Pew Research Center 2014). As Waters and Pineau (2015) note, the high proportion of Catholic new immigrants is not surprising given the range of countries that are represented by new immigrants to the United States. In addition, as in the early years of Catholics coming to the United States, many immigrant Catholics today also live in poverty. Almost half of all Catholics in California have annual family incomes less than thirty thousand dollars, and 55 percent are first-generation immigrants (Pew Research Center 2014).

Some argue that because discrimination against Catholics is no longer an issue, Catholic schools are not needed. Indeed, research on the academic outcomes of children who attend Catholic K–12 schools compared to other private and public schools finds that when controlling for social class and race, students in Catholic schools do not do markedly better, except those living in poor neighborhoods where the public schools tend to be low-performing (Huchting et al. 2014; Neal 1997). This is the context in which Saint Middle School, the school that students profiled in this book attended from sixth grade to eighth, was founded.

In this book we follow the educational trajectories of students from four graduating eighth-grade cohorts until they are young adults.[6] Saint purposely involves parents from the mainly low-income, primarily Spanish-speaking neighborhood. The purposeful structure and staffing at Saint help students feel supported in their educational aspirations by their families, the school staff, and teachers, as well as by the neighborhood.

As discussed previously, the school is connected to a thriving church—a church first founded for first-generation Italian immigrants. Low-income white Catholics whose families immigrated many generations ago are now less likely to attend church than their first-generation ancestors. Instead, white Catholic churchgoers today are more likely to be middle- and high-income (Schwadel, McCarthy, and Nelsen 2009). Catholic schools are also represented by this demographic. This pattern does not hold true for Latina/o Catholics, however, for whom ethnic parishes have grown, and low-income Latina/o families have high rates of church attendance. Even though Catholic churches play an important role in the lives of Latina/o families, especially those who are first- and second-generation immigrants, recent books about Latina/o students do not include discussions about the role of religion (Nelson 2017; Ovink 2017), perhaps because religion is more salient in the lives of parents than for their second-generation children.

Latina/o Children in California. In California just over half of all children under age twenty are Latina/o, and they make up 55 percent of all students in California's K–12 public school system. Only 5 percent of Latina/o children were not born in the United States, a full 95 percent are U.S. citizens, and most attend public schools. In addition, nearly one million Latina/o students are in California's public colleges and universities (Education Trust–West 2017). In 2004, Latinas/os made up over 60 percent of all second-generation immigrants in California (Ramakrishnan and Johnson 2005). This is a very sizeable proportion of the population in the state and children in the education system. Only 27 percent of Latina/o students in the California county where this study took place meet or exceed state standards for mathematics, compared to 69 percent of whites, and only 37 percent meet or exceed the state standards for English (76 percent of whites do). These realities are colliding with state concerns that there will not be enough educated adults to fill the future occupational demands in the state. As a result, understanding the experiences of Latina/o students and their trajectories through schools on the path to college can help address issues the state and country face in graduating more first-generation students with a college degree.

The students profiled in this book allow us to understand the experiences of students who are a transitional generation by starting with the experiences of students at one school, Saint Middle School, that does not separate family, religion, or education but instead addresses the full context of students' lives. By employing staff and structuring the school to address the realities of transitional generations, Saint actively involves both parents and students in the school. Martha, a second-generation immigrant and graduate of Saint, talks about how Saint Middle differed from her public elementary school and later her private high school, especially related to the involvement of her parents:

> I've always seen parents struggle with their kids because of the language barrier. During my elementary school years, I would have to translate from my teacher to my parents. And then at Saint it was just like my teachers could talk directly to my parents because they spoke the same language and it was just so much easier. And in high school, again, it was like my parents weren't involved because conferences were optional. I never really told my parents about conferences because I was like, "It's just going to be a struggle to get a translator or for me to translate everything that's happening." And I think that's when my parents stopped being so involved in my school life. I think they wanted to be involved obviously, they would ask to see my books, how school was going and all that. It's just so much harder to get them involved.

The transitions between different schools necessitated that Martha begin to make independent decisions about her schooling much earlier than her CGC peers. This caused many students who were both FGC and second-generation immigrants to prematurely hasten their transition to adulthood.

Transitioning to Adulthood

The transition to adulthood has also been referred to as "the time in between," in between adolescence and the restrictions that are often imposed by school and family, to a time of emergence into the responsibilities of adulthood (Arnett 2015).[7] Legally students gain an increasing amount of rights and responsibilities, typically work and date more, and begin to transition out of the homes of their families and think about starting their own families. Today this time of life, what Arnett (2015) calls "emerging adulthood," occurs over a longer time frame than in the past, usually lasting from age eighteen to twenty-nine.

For those who enroll in college directly out of high school, they are also experiencing transitioning to adulthood while still a student. The structure and culture of colleges are often based on the assumption that students need a growing amount of freedom, within some limits. Part of this transition to adulthood that is often encouraged is the idea of "going away to college." As we have discussed, living away from parents for the first time to attend school full-time has been considered the traditional college path that not only helps students increase their individual human capital but also provides a safe space where young adults can become more independent from their parents (Wartman and Savage 2008). CGC students are much more likely than FGC students to live on campus (Engle and Tinto 2008). However, an increasing percentage of students are living at home while in college to save money (Sallie Mae 2018).

Whether students move away from home or not for college, the growing need for schooling beyond high school has extended the involvement of parents in their children's lives as they move into and even through early adulthood (Hamilton 2016). The growing phenomenon of children going away to college and then returning to live at home (the boomerang effect) is generally presented as one of financial necessity, on the part of the child. Demographers wonder then how to define adulthood and what conditions determine when one is an adult. As we will see from the experiences of the FGC students profiled here, going to college locally and continuing to live at home was based on financial necessity, not only for themselves, but also for their families. More understanding about how social class influences discourse about the transition to adulthood is needed.

Transitioning from adolescence to young adulthood is seen as a particularly important time in the life of immigrant children (Paat 2013), especially for those who have played a crucial role in helping parents adjust to a new culture. A healthy transition into adulthood can result in young adults being able to deal more readily with changes and challenges (Portes and Rumbaut 2001; Waters et al. 2010), and schools can be part of what drives a healthy transition. For young adults who are undocumented, the transition to adulthood brings new challenges. While students who are undocumented are protected in the public K–12 school system, when they graduate from high school and turn eighteen they are suddenly responsible for their own legal status, what Roberto Gonzales refers to as a process of "learning to be illegal" (2011, 2016). Most Saint students are not undocumented; only five of the fifty-one alumni from Saint interviewed for this project referred to themselves as DACA or DREAMer students. However, many more students had parents who were undocumented. This presented additional issues in transitioning to adulthood and making decisions about college when the threat of possible deportation of parents might increase their responsibilities to their siblings and other family members. In chapter 5 we will see how that impacted the stability of families, which in turn influenced students' paths after high school.

Transitioning to Different Schools

For most students, the path to college involves transitioning between many different schools. The typical student has at least four school transitions: preschool to elementary school, elementary to middle school, middle to high school, and high school to college. However, this is true only if students do not move or change schools. Further complicating this picture, the United States has many different levels of schools and types of schools, and then drastically different qualities of schools within each type.

All of these differences mean that education, one of the most important institutions in the twenty-first century, is difficult to study. There are multiple selection issues related to which students attend which schools. So by the time we conduct studies of inequality among college students, there are already many students who are missing from our research. Those most likely to be missing are those who never enrolled in college, attend part-time, or frequently drop in and out of college. We have excellent and very interesting books about what happens to students in college by social class status or between those of different classes or based on differences in experiences between students at different types of colleges, but there are few that follow students through their full educational trajectories, on all the paths that they take.[8] Some exceptions are *When Grit Isn't Enough* by Linda Nathan, who interviewed alumni from a public arts high school about what happens to them after they graduate. Megan Holland's *Divergent Paths to College* and Patricia McDonough's *Choosing Colleges* show how different types of high schools structure the college application and choice process.[9] This book is similar, but starts earlier in the trajectories of aspiring FGC students, examining their elementary schools and controlling for many selection issues by focusing on students with similar characteristics who all went to the same middle school.[10]

For the first-generation and low-income students profiled in this book, the path to college included interfacing with many different types of public and private institutions. Isabel, whom we met in chapter 1, attended Saint Middle and then a Catholic single-sex high school where she received a scholarship toward the almost nineteen-thousand-dollar tuition. Isabel's chances of attending a four-year college after high school were increased because of the high school she attended. But there were many challenges to staying on the college path for Isabel, even with the advantage of having attended a high school that aims to send all of its graduates to college.

It is essential to understand this particular group of potential FGC students because they are academically able to attend college, but still face hurdles to accomplishing a college degree. In table 2.1 we can compare Saint students to national samples of students who have at least one parent with a bachelor's degree (CGC), those whose parents have at most a high school degree (FGC), and, within the FGC group, those who also identify as Latina/o. Nationally, while 33 percent of CGC students go to a private school, only 9 percent of FGC students attend private high schools, and only 5 percent of FGC who are also Latina/o attend such schools. First-generation students are very likely to attend high schools that have a high proportion of students from poor families, and few students graduate and go on to four-year colleges. While almost 70 percent of CGC students went to high schools where half or more of students went on to four-year colleges, only 26 percent of FGC Latina/o students attended high schools with students likely to go on to four-year schools. This is different for the high proportion of Saint alumni who attend private Catholic high schools in which almost all students go on to college.

The last column in table 2.1 allows us to compare students nationally to alumni from Saint. Saint alumni are much more likely than the national sample of Latina/o FGC students to attend private high schools, which means they are more likely to be in schools where most of their classmates go to college. Yet because California does not yet have a good system to track students post–high school, these data are incomplete (Zinshteyn 2018). As the last two columns show, Latina/o FGC students are more likely to be in schools where more than 50 percent of the student body receives a free lunch, signaling a level of inequality that likely affects other resources available to students for further education.

Saint alumni are also much more likely than the national sample of FGC to take the traditional path to college of going to a four-year school away from home. Because Saint alumni went to different types of high schools, we have the opportunity to consider how type of school influences outcomes. This is an important area of interest given the push by some policy makers to fix inequity between schools by providing students and families with more flexibility to choose from a larger number of schools.

Table 2.1
Comparing CGC and FGC Nationally and to Saint Alumni

	CGC National Sample ($n = 6{,}711$)	FGC National Sample ($n = 4{,}270$)	FGC & Latina/o National Sample ($n = 944$)	Saint Alum Four Cohorts ($n = 154$)
Catholic HS (%)	17.6	5.5	4.2	58.6
Other private HS (%)	15.2	3.2	1.2	0.4
Parents expect BA (%)	94.8	77.5	82.0	—
Attend HS 50%+ students get free lunch (%)	9.2	27.9	44.7	38.0
Attend HS 50%+ students go to 4-year college (%)	68.7	37.7	25.7	—
Any postsecondary (%)	94.6	74.2	72.1	82.0
No postsecondary (%)	5.4	25.8	27.9	18.0
Of those who went to college: In college; live with parents (%)	18.6	50.3	65.0	64.0
Traditional college (4-year; don't live with parents) (%)	56.8	20.2	10.8	30.0

NOTE: Dash indicates no data available.

Public and Charter Schools in the United States

Like their parents and grandparents before them, most students in the United States attend a traditional public school. But in urban areas there are many different types of schools, especially if parents have the necessary financial resources to send their children to schools not near their homes.

At the time of this writing, the U.S. Department of Education is actively touting a "school choice" model as a means to address inequity in public schools. School choice initiatives often pit schools in communities against one another (Darling-Hammond and Lieberman 2012; Meier and Gasoi 2017). In particular, the growth of charter schools, starting in the early 1990s, has helped fuel discussions of school choice as a solution for fixing underperforming public schools. Charter schools are public schools, but families must apply and acceptances must be determined by a lottery system. However, charter schools are not required to accept students midyear and do not have to follow the same regulations as traditional public schools, including provisions for students with special needs. Nationally, charter schools have shown mixed results, and outcomes vary greatly by region (Center for Research on Education Outcomes [CREDO] 2015; Hill, Angel, and Christensen 2006).

Beyond charter schools, another school choice model involves providing parents with vouchers that they can use to pay for private or public schools. Proponents of school choice and voucher programs argue that because private schools tend to have better rates of college enrollment and graduation, more students should have access to them. However, the success rates of private schools are often driven by the social class of the families who can afford to attend. Regardless, some pilot state-level programs to provide families with vouchers have been developed. A study examining the college enrollment rates of students who participated in Florida's statewide high school voucher program found that students who attended private elementary and/or secondary schools were more likely than a comparison group of similar students to attend college (Chingos and Kuehn 2017); however most of the college enrollment was in two-year colleges, where many FGC students enroll mainly because of perceived lower cost. Community colleges often have low rates of retention, graduation, and transfer to four-year schools. In this book we can examine these issues more closely because about half of Saint alumni attended private high schools and the other half attended traditional public or charter high schools.

Private Schools

While the public school system in the United States has increasingly become segregated by social class, private schools primarily serve wealthy students. And students in private schools are the most likely to come from families where two generations or more (grandparents and parents) have college degrees.

Today private Catholic high schools and colleges charge very high tuitions and are populated mainly by students from families who can afford the tuition. In response, and recognizing that Catholic schools today do not cater to the most recent cohorts of new immigrant students who are low-income, new networks of Catholic schools have been created to fill in that gap and provide Catholic school options to those who would be the first in their families to attend college. Saint was formed with this intention, following the Nativity school model.

In 1971, the first Nativity middle school was started (Fenzel 2009); now there is a wide network. As of 2008 there were sixty-four Nativity-modeled middle schools across twenty-seven states, all focused on educating students who are low-income, who are usually first- or second-generation immigrants, whose families identify as Catholic, and who would be the first in their families to attend college. Schools in the Nativity network are strategically located in neighborhoods with high rates of poverty with no or underperforming middle schools. As a result, Nativity schools usually have many more students apply than are accepted.

Nativity schools have as their common mission breaking the cycle of poverty via education. The schools and classes are small, there is an extended day and year, and school staff continue to provide support to their alumni after graduation. As a group, Nativity schools have high graduation rates and work to place students in appropriate high schools, including Catholic schools. For the 2016 graduates of Nativity schools across the United States, over 60 percent enrolled in private high schools (NMC 2018). At private schools there is a separate admissions process. This creates a selection effect that is very difficult to control for in determining outcomes.[11]

Saint has a process of checking in with their alumni at least once a year to chronicle their educational progress and work experiences. These data, for all students who graduated eighth grade from 2004 to 2013, are presented in table 2.2. The analysis allows us to examine the outcomes of Saint alumni by the type of high school they attended. Looking at the rates of college enrollment by high school type, we see that that alumni who went to private high schools after graduating from Saint were much more likely to attend college, especially four-year colleges. Overall, since graduating from high school, 34 percent had enrolled in a public four-year college, 14 percent in a four-year private, 27 percent in a two-year public, and 2 percent in a for-

Table 2.2
Post–High School Trajectories by Type of High School (Saint Alumni 2004–2013) ($N = 245$)[a]

Post-HS Trajectory	Public HS ($n = 74$)	Charter HS ($n = 44$)	Single-Sex Private Catholic HS ($n = 94$)	Coed Private Catholic HS ($n = 33$)
4-year public college (%)	10	43	45	52
4-year private college (%)	1	2	27	27
2-year college (%)	35	34	20	12
For-profit college (%)	1	5	2	0
Working; no postsecondary (%)	45	16	5	9
Military (%)	8	0	1	0

[a] Any college enrollment is captured here, even if not currently enrolled (alumni activities last update spring 2017).

profit; 20 percent never enrolled and were working; and 3 percent were in the military.

Saint worked to academically prepare students and to help them apply to private Catholic schools that are known to be very academically rigorous and also send most, if not all, of their students to college. Looking at what happens to FGC Saint alumni through different types of high schools allows us to understand potholes on the path to college for students who are academically able, are motivated, and who have parents who support their educational goals.

Conclusion

This book takes a local, regional approach to understand the experiences of aspiring FGC students over time. "A regional focus is necessary because a traditional model of linear college attendance at a single institution does not provide an accurate framework through which to understand the complex postsecondary patterns of nontraditional students and students who attend commuter institutions" (Ziskin et al. 2010, 73). We need more research specifically focused on FGC students at two-year colleges and other types of institutions, where most FGC students begin their postsecondary work (see Goldrick-Rab 2010; Inman and Mayes 1999; Pascarella et al. 2003; Ryken 2006). *The Journey Before Us* highlights what happens to students who take a number of different journeys through the educational system and interrogates what FGC students need and the factors that cut across all the paths.

In the next chapter we look at the transition of students from their elementary school to attending Saint Middle as well as their experiences transitioning from Saint Middle to different types of high schools. These transitions provide background to help us understand why students ultimately take the college paths they do and what schools, communities, and policy makers can do to improve the college-going trajectories of prospective FGC students.

3

Middle and High School Transitions and Experiences on the Path to College

————————————————•

> I didn't really have an innocence when
> I was a child because I was already
> exposed to drugs and gangs in elemen-
> tary school. I would have had a different
> lifestyle if I wouldn't have gone to Saint.
> They kept us so busy with school,
> summer camp, and summer school.
> —Veronica

Looking back at her experience at Saint Middle School, Veronica is grateful for that time in her life and realizes that even though things did not turn
out as she had hoped after she graduated, Saint showed her the many options
available to her. Veronica's educational journey started at the same public
elementary school attended by most Saint students. The school was walking distance from the small apartment Veronica shared with her family. She

knew of Saint from her older brother who attended. She excelled at the school, which she described as "such a family place." Middle school was a time of feeling supported, growing in her academic abilities and potential, and feeling taken care of. "Saint does a great job with you knowing that they are there for their students. . . . I learned what a teacher really is from them." Veronica also credits Saint with exposing her to high schools that she would have never known about.

Veronica got into and attended Cardinal, a private Catholic high school known for its academics and sports teams as well as its high tuition. While the academic adjustment was not difficult, socially and emotionally Veronica struggled: "In middle school everyone felt the same and I didn't feel discriminated against in any way. Everyone else had the same situations: parents who were undocumented, no money, lived in the same area. It was very easy to connect with everybody. But high school was completely different. It was difficult because there were so many people that didn't understand what I went through. I was used to going to a school with people who looked like me. I wasn't used to people who didn't have financial problems or problems at home."

Veronica did not find the academic work in high school too difficult; Saint had prepared her well. She returned to Saint almost every day after school for the first two years of high school to do her homework with other Saint alumni. Veronica wanted to get involved in activities, but Cardinal was "a big sports school, and I didn't have any background in sports, so there was no room for me. And then I tried to join the robotics club, but you had to go in there already knowing a lot of math. But I really enjoyed my science classes in high school." The high school was far from her house, but her full scholarship included a bus pass, so although it was over an hour bus ride, it allowed her to make it to school each day. While in school she did a lot of "under-the-table jobs" in catering companies and also worked at Jamba Juice to support herself and help her parents send money to family in Mexico. "Money was always kind of a problem in my family, plus my family in Mexico was also economically challenged." So although the school work was not too difficult, "I had other problems going on so it was distracting and I couldn't really focus [on school]."

Veronica continued to feel isolated from other students, and during her junior year she began to think that a teacher thought she was stealing food from the cafeteria. She wore her hoodie and kept to herself. Leading into her senior year she experienced multiple traumatic events outside of school that caused her to stop having contact with her family. She became homeless but kept attending classes. When asked if she told any of her teachers or the counselor she was close to what was going on, she said, "I didn't know what to say. I didn't tell them at school. I didn't tell anyone at school. I didn't want to tell my teacher about all [that was going on]. I asked for more time for homework, I told her one thing that had happened, but I didn't want to just make excuses or ask for extra favors. It was just tough. I didn't know what to say, I didn't know how to reach out. I wanted to deal on my own." Now she looks back on that time and realizes she should have reached out for help: "I want to tell others that they can ask for help. They don't have to do it alone. It's okay to get help."

Veronica applied to and was accepted by some colleges, but at that point she had no contact with her family and filling out the financial aid forms was too difficult. Even though she wanted to go to college, she said financially it was not an option.

Veronica's experience raises many issues that arose for students as they were accepted to and then transitioned into attending Saint and then again as they transitioned from Saint to high school. These factors also made a difference in students' ability to do well in high school and as they were thinking about applying to college.

Saint put students on the path to college in middle school by certifying for students that they were academically able and could learn difficult material. They also let students know that if they worked hard they could get into the best private high schools in the community, which would pave the way to college and ultimately break the cycle of poverty experienced by their families. But as we will see in this and the following chapters, reality was different from the hope for many Saint students, especially the transition to high school from Saint.

This chapter focuses on middle and high school transitions starting with the adjustment to Saint and then as students move on to high school. The high school transition includes adjusting to academics as well as to available supports depending on the type of high school students attended, differences in the level of culture shock related to the dominant race/ethnicity and social class of most other students at their high school, how the circumstances and needs of their families influenced their educational trajectory, and the role that middle and high school teachers and counselors played in their transition to high school and as students were thinking of their next transition post–high school graduation.

Transitioning to Middle School

Researchers have questioned the potential harm of the middle school model in the United States, particularly issues associated with transitioning students to what is typically a larger school during a sensitive developmental time in their lives. Holas and Huston (2012) found that boys in particular had a lowered connection to school after they transitioned to middle school and that size and quality of the instruction were major factors in determining the smoothness of the transition. Saint attempted to mitigate these types of issues by maintaining a small school (about 150 students total in sixth through eighth grades) and classroom environment, partnering with family, and having an extended day and year that kept the main focus on academics (Fenzel 2009). Asked about the transition to Saint from her public elementary school and the differences between the two schools, Jeanne said, "I think it was just because it was public to private. Public schools I guess are more lenient. I don't know if that's the right word, but private school is more intimate and they really check on you and see how you are doing with everything. So, I think that was the biggest change for us."

At first most Saint students were not excited about attending Saint. Students knew that the school days were long and that the academic expectations were rigorous. They also did not like having to go to a school that was different from the public middle school that their friends were attending. Said Alex,

> As a fifth grader [I was thinking] that was going to be a lot of school for me. I mean, knowing that I was going to be in school from seven A.M. to six P.M. So, going in there, I was like what am I going to do for all this time there? My feelings about this were the same the whole time I went there. But I kind of just kept going. All these [other] kids are like getting out at two thirty and we are getting out at six. I mean, I didn't get past it, but I got used to it. . . . What they did is get us into a routine, where like every day you're going to have this for one-hour, two-hour period where you do homework and that was from five to six before we got out. . . . It really got me into this groove where you've got responsibilities to do and you have to plan and all that stuff.

Students carried this routine into high school, first with required, supported homework periods their first year and then as part of their independent routine as they got further along in school.

Beyond the long school days, students also had to get used to the rigor of the academics as well as the amount of time they were expected to devote to academics. For these alumni, Saint did not offer any extracurricular activities.[1] And while they had recess where they could play, there were no organized sports or clubs.

Another part of the experience of attending Saint was required summer school. This included both a sleep-away camp as well as summer courses at one of the local private Catholic high schools. The students said that the summer camp was instrumental in their social transition to Saint. Said Alex, "You go to this camp before you go into school and you get to meet people there. So, by the time you go into school, you know people from that. And then by the end of it, by the end of graduation, I knew everybody pretty well. I was pretty close with everyone. So that's one thing that it does right is that it has such small classes that you know everyone on a personal level." About the adjustment to Saint, Danielle said, "It was very good because before entering the school they had summer camp and it was very nice because it's where you got to meet your classmates and you met all those in the summer class too and it was a way to bring the community together."

For most Saint students, summer camp was the first time they slept away from home and they were nervous about the whole experience of camp. Having to do things that were new and scary and being able to "push through and do them" were important for shaping Yesenia's ability to do new and difficult things later in her educational trajectory: "I had never been hiking or swimming, so it was very difficult the first camp, the first year. But I feel that because of those experiences, I am who I am today. I never would have done those things if it wasn't for Saint. So, I'm very grateful for that."

About the summer courses at a private high school, Alex said, "And every year in the summer we go to St. John's and we take summer courses. It's mandatory, and that gives us something to do over the summer and that is very helpful. It got us into the atmosphere and what those kinds of schools are." Anthony represented the sentiment of many alumni who said that Saint "taught me that every day is a chance to learn. I love that Saint taught me that and that that is the way you are going to break the cycle, and I've become such an interesting person because I have let myself go there."

Although Saint focused mostly on academics and on preparing and transitioning students to go to good high schools, the school did start exposing students to the idea of going to college. Alumni would come back and talk about their paths to college, and the director of graduate support also did summer sessions on applying to college for both students and their parents. These were attended by current students as well as graduates. Joseph said that it was the college pendants and posters up in the halls and rooms at Saint that made an impression on him: "Saint had colleges up and that's how I got the names and started getting curious as to what they were and you know, the different levels and I started learning about the UCs, CSUs, and all the great universities around here. So, Saint and College Prep Charter definitely made college more familiar to me."

"School Choice" and High School

When the alumni at Saint were graduating from middle school there were no public high schools in their neighborhood. Most students attended one of eight different high schools. These high schools varied quite a bit: two were traditional public schools, one was a charter school, and five were private Catholic schools (two of these were coed, two were single-sex female, and one was single-sex male). Because of the work that Saint staff did with the private high schools so Saint students could receive financial support if accepted, Saint helped students apply to at least one private school. The graduate support director and other Saint staff talked with students about which school they thought matched their academic abilities and interests, and students also attended "shadow" days at any of the schools they wanted to before deciding where to apply. To help students get further perspectives on the schools, Saint alumni came back to talk to seventh- and eighth-graders about their high school experiences, and students also met tutors from the various high schools (some of whom were Saint alumni) during homework time after school.

During the time that these alumni attended Saint they were allowed to apply to just one of the private options. If too many students in the graduating cohort wanted to attend the same school, some of the students were told to pick a different school. Now Saint allows students to apply to more than one private school, and the sorting-out process happens at the financial aid stage in an attempt to provide at least some support to all students who are accepted. Because parents' knowledge of the high school options for their children was limited, Saint staff played a significant role in directing students in their high school choices.

Some students felt that they had freedom to choose which private school they wanted to apply to; others felt that Saint directed their choice more than they wished. Juana was encouraged by Saint to attend a public high school, even though she desired a private high school. She was told her grades were not strong enough and that there were not scholarships for everyone from Saint who wanted to apply to private school. Juana got into the lottery at College Prep Charter, where her brother also went. She recognized that going to College Prep would be "a perfect fit because all of us come from the same background, just like at [Saint]." It was also much smaller than the other high schools. But she also knew that College Prep had only a few AP courses and that all of the students took the same classes for the most part, a difference from the private school she was interested in.

Students could afford private high school only if they received a scholarship, which was not guaranteed. Students realized that some schools had more scholarships available than others and that their parents might be asked to pay more if they wanted to attend one of the schools with fewer scholarships. Said Danielle, who was raised by her grandmother and did not apply to any of the private high schools, "But then I knew money was always tight. So, I knew like going to a private high school is not—it's more expensive than here, of course. And I kind of like always reminded her like, oh well, I mean—I'm not the best student. So, I always told [my grandmother] like, 'I won't guarantee you that I'd be able to get a scholarship or something to pay for school.' So, I told her, 'You know what, Presidential Public was always our family school. So that's the school I'm going to."

In the era of "school choice," eight schools seem like a lot. But the reality is that for the private schools, the schools choose the students, not the other way around. Further, the public options are mandated by where students live. Those who stayed in the neighborhood where Saint was located were assigned to one of two traditional public high schools a few miles from the neighborhood. At that time, College Prep Charter was also outside the community but has since moved and is now the closest public high school to Saint. The Catholic schools are of varying distances from Saint.

Veronica decided that she liked Cardinal Private, a coed Catholic school, and she was admitted to that school with a full, four-year scholarship. The tuition for Cardinal was close to twenty thousand dollars a year. If she would not have attended Cardinal she would have attended her assigned public high school, Presidential Public.

Table 3.1 shows general characteristics of the high schools that most students from Saint attended as well as the variation in the number of students and ratio of students to teachers at each school. The schools for which there are limited data show another problem with school choice models: private schools are not required to report the same level and types of data as public schools. The capitalist model of "school choice" presumes that the market will correct any problems at the schools. However, the lack of ability to compare schools leaves parents at a disadvantage, especially those who might not be in social circles where the quality of private schools is discussed and the pros and cons are debated.

A bigger issue was that the characteristics of Saint differed from those of the high schools as well as the public middle schools. All of the students felt safe and protected in the small atmosphere at Saint. Isabel, whom we first met in chapter 1, found Saint to be a place where she and her family could feel comfortable and get help. The principal bought Isabel and her sister their very first new clothes. The teachers at Saint helped her discover her academic strengths, and the structure of the small classes combined with the required homework club after school helped her to stay on track. Alex also talked about the staff treating him like family and that the principal at Saint was a "father figure" for him and many Saint students: "He would joke around, he made dad jokes. He would do that. He'd always be generous to everyone. He'd check up on people. That was always nice." While Saint tried to prepare students for the different atmosphere in high school, students said it was difficult to understand what it would be like until they were actually at school. This transition will be discussed next.

High School Transitions

Academic Transitions

Students made an assessment about the academic rigor of their high school early, usually within the first week of school. All Saint alumni said that Saint prepared them very well for the academic expectations they faced in high school. A few students said that they wished there was more lab science at Saint, but otherwise they felt able to write well, take notes, and excel in their classes of all subjects. The goal of Saint to prepare students for the academic rigor of private college-preparatory high schools was successful. But the consistent stress on academics resulted in two different outcomes in the academic transition to high school depending on the type of high school Saint students attended.

Table 3.1
Characteristics of High Schools Attended, High School Graduates Class of 2016

High School	Total Student Body	# 12th Grade	Students per Teacher[a]	% Latina/o	% Low- income	% UC/CSU Eligible	% SAT ≥ 1500/ ACT ≥ 21	# Students per Counselor
Presidential Public	1,903	377	22.3	73	61	55	33/56	634
Village Public	1,697	361	22.4	54	42	45	56/66	566
College Prep Charter	334	74	20.1	93	89	82	—/24	—
St. Cate's Private[b]	630	149	13.9	16	—	100	—	—
St Theresa's Private[b]	750	223	12.7	14	—	100	—	—
St. John's Private[c]	1,647	384	20.6	—	—	100	—	—
Cardinal Private[c]	1,727	423	19.4	—	—	100	—	—
Mountain Private[b]	1,755	422	16.4	11	—	100	—	—

NOTE: Dash indicates no data available.

SOURCE: Data collected for the 2015–2016 school year or for the class of 2016 when those data were collected the following year. Public school data are from the School Accountability Report Card (SARC) and the California Department of Education DataQuest website: https://data1.cde.ca.gov/dataquest/.

[a] "The pupil-teacher ratio is the total student enrollment divided by the number of full-time-equivalent teachers. The number of pupils per teacher is smaller than the average class size, which is the number of pupils attending divided by the number of classes. Some teachers have special assignments in a school or in the district and so are not confined to one subject or one classroom." www.ed-data.org/article/Teachers-in-California.

[b] Private school data are for those schools that provided data for NCES's PSS Private School Universe Survey data for the 2015–2016 school year. See https://nces.ed.gov /surveys/pss/ and https://nces.ed.gov/surveys/pss/privateschoolsearch/.

[c] Data are from the Private School Directory for 2015–2016 collected by the California Department of Education.

For those attending private high schools, students said that their schools were challenging but similar to Saint, and they felt able to do the work. Some students would return to Saint for help with their homework, especially their first year of high school, but they became more confident asking their high school teachers for help as their time there increased. However, the academic rigor of Saint worked in unexpected ways for students who attended public high schools.

All of the students who attended public high schools (traditional public and charters) mentioned how "easy" academically their transition to high school was. Although grades in middle school were usually the reason they did not apply, were not accepted, or did not receive financial aid at a private high school, they still were very well prepared for a rigorous high school curriculum. But at their public high school, at least at the start of their first year, they found a "dumbed-down curriculum." Said Danielle,

> Academically, I felt like my first year I was doing very well and all. But because here at [Saint], they tend to teach us a year higher in private schools I've noticed. So, when I entered as a freshman [at Presidential Public], I was like, "Oh! I know everything." I knew this and I knew that. I was passing all my classes. But then, you know, I started to slack off. And so, coming the next year, so it was kind of like, "Oh! I'm slacking off." And it was just getting so much harder because in the private school, they're teaching you a year ahead. . . . And then in the public school, I noticed there wasn't that structure and the teachers were more of like—this is your education, you're doing it if you want to do it. They weren't as supportive. So, it just kind of depended who you got as well.

All of the students from Saint Middle had learned how to succeed academically and had their expectations for their own educations raised. This was true even for students who did not excel academically while at Saint. When they went to high school they expected the same level of rigor and high expectations. However, those Saint students who attended traditional public or charter high schools found teachers who they perceived as having lowered expectations. Said Chris, "They treated us like we were stupid." In response, as Danielle said, students "slacked off." They did not really have much homework, especially compared to Saint, and they used their after-school time to hang out with their friends. The students attended classes, did the minimal work, and did fine the first semester, but then their grades started to decline. Once they reached their second year of high school the work got harder, and then they were too far behind to pull the kinds of grades to stay on a path to college.

Chris talked further about his experience at a public school after not getting into the private high school he wanted to attend. He was surprised and defeated when he did not get into Cardinal, especially because his brother did. Shame set in for many students who were not accepted to any of the private high schools while they watched their friends from Saint be admitted and attend. Students in this situation said they wished they would have fully understood how important their middle school grades were and also started to doubt their academic abilities after all. Chris attended College Prep Charter. He did well the first semester, because it was so easy, a repeat of what he had done in eighth grade. But by the second semester he was not doing well academically, and in his sophomore year the principal from Saint came and met with Chris and his high school advisor. Chris felt both appreciation for the concern his former principal had for him and embarrassment that he was doing so badly and had "let him down." After that he avoided people who reached out to him from Saint, and he dropped out of high school. Later he went to a different public high school for two years and graduated, motivated to provide a good example for his younger siblings as both of his older siblings had dropped out of high school.

Martinez and Deil-Amen (2015, 28) explored the issue of academic rigor in schools for Latina/o students. They found that students struggled their first year of college if the rigor of their high schools was not adequate: "The multifaceted concept of academic rigor includes course content and instruction that challenges students to operate above their grade level, incorporates an extensive and demanding workload, and overall, calls for high expectations from all school actors." Saint students experienced this type of rigor while at Saint. If they attended a private high school that rigor was continued, but Saint alumni who attended the public and charter high schools saw a drop in rigor the first semester. Then they said they "messed around," "did the minimum," "did not take school seriously," and "hung around with friends" instead of concentrating on school.

Ironically, although the public high schools that Saint students attended had low college enrollment of their graduates, students at public high schools in poorer neighborhoods considered the public schools that most Saint students attended (Presidential and Village Public) "rich" schools. One Saint alumnus said that her cousins asked her for college information because they heard that Presidential Public talked about college more than their school.

An alumnus who attended Presidential said that in her junior year she realized that there were really two schools within her high school, the "poor school" that she attended with other Latinas and then a totally different school where all "the white students were." She advocated for herself and worked hard to get into Advanced Placement (AP) courses and ended up going to and graduating from a selective college.

As Lewis and Diamond (2015) note in their comprehensive study of a highly ranked public high school, even attending a high-quality public school is not enough for all students to succeed. The authors saw how stratification by race and class affected students and resulted in very different postgraduation trajectories based on characteristics they could not control. The design of high schools, even though they seemed "race neutral," resulted in what Lewis and Diamond said were unintentional consequences for students based on race. The authors also noted that "opportunity hoarding" by white families within the school was a major contributor to differential academic outcomes by race. The main structural differences were in how discipline policies were enacted and tracking practices that resulted in opportunity hoarding in valued programs that provided access to honors and advanced courses. Further, white parents justified the current system and opposed changes that might have opened up access to a greater diversity of students. This resulted in stratification within schools, not just between them.

Students also experienced family situations that jeopardized their academic trajectories. Isabel was admitted to St. Theresa with a scholarship but had to leave her sophomore year and move suddenly to Southern California, attending a public school there for part of her sophomore year. When she moved back to Northern California she was not allowed to return to the private school as only a few weeks remained in the school year, so she attended Village Public. She found Village very different from St. Theresa and asked to return for her junior year. She was granted admittance, but the move disrupted her schooling and her momentum as a student: "Before the move I got through high school really easy, it was really nice. And then, after the move, because my sophomore year was kind of messy, it wasn't quite as easy to keep up with the schoolwork. . . . So it was difficult academically after the move, socially it was okay. But I was working at my internship, helping my mom, and had a pretty big responsibility over my [three] siblings too."

In terms of how students stayed on track academically, they said that the required homework time after school when they were at Saint helped to discipline them to continue the practice of doing homework right after school, even after they transitioned to high school. Saint initially required their high school student alumni to return to the school to do their homework and get support. However, many of the private high schools wanted to provide this level of assistance to students and instead created their own homework support centers with a staff person who worked with Saint alum. Samuel said that his mom had the support person at St. John's "on speed dial" and was always checking in with her about his grades. When that high school support person spoke Spanish, it made it easier for more Saint students' parents to be involved in their high school experience.

While some students found this extra support at their high school helpful, others felt they did not need it, and at some schools Saint alumni reported after school to the same room as the "detention kids," which was embarrassing. The requirement also limited their ability to participate in after-school and cocurricular activities. Students who have graduated from Saint more recently have the option to return there after school if they want to work on their homework, but it is not required. And the high schools do not mandate that students do their homework at school all four years. Many students said that they found being able to return to Saint helpful, especially during their first semester and year of high school. They felt comfortable there, and it was easier for them to ask for help with their homework there than at their high school.

Social Transitions and Culture Shock

One of the main reasons returning to Saint was helpful to alumni during the first year of high school was because of the culture shock that students experienced transitioning from middle school to their high school. This was particularly the case when students attended private schools. Saint students came from public elementary schools and their middle school, where the other students looked and lived like them. Many had parents who spoke mainly Spanish, and all came from low-income families. Then they found themselves in classrooms where they "were the only Latino" for the first time. At the beginning of this chapter, Veronica talked about the isolation that she felt being so different from the rest of the students in her high school. The students who felt this noted that they appreciated the ability to go to a school that they knew as an expensive, private, and "good school." But the social differences were difficult to prepare for and adjust to.

Usually these experiences occurred the first day or week of school and persisted. Sofía talked about her first day of high school when she was asked by sophomores in her biology class, "'Do you speak Mexican?' and I was like, 'what?' So I just experienced a lot of microaggressions, but I was too young to figure out what I was going through and why I was feeling like I was." Tony mentioned his experience adjusting from middle school to his private Catholic high school:

> It was different because in middle school everyone is Mexican, but in high school there are different people. During my first week of high school we were in religion talking about our family backgrounds and I was sharing and realized that people didn't understand what I was saying about my family's traditions. Wow, it was shocking. Well I just, that was like, it made me realize that I was in a different place, because before I was like these are just people. I didn't really look into like, "you're white, you're black, or this," it was just like, "you're a person," but after that [experience] I realized they were different. So, I was more careful about what I said after that. My parents, family, private things, I would have shared it at my middle school, but not now, never mind.

Tony defined the experience not as "bad" but as "different" and dealt with this new way of thinking of himself and his classmates by saying that he was unique: "I can help people in Spanish, they see me as a friend." Later that first year he had a similar experience: "Another time we were hanging out in the cafeteria and we were just foolin' around, looking up people's addresses on Google Earth. All the other guys had these big houses, but when they looked up mine they said. 'Wow you live there?' It just shocked them, but they didn't make fun of it they were just like, 'Wow.'"

Anthony spent his first year in high school keeping to himself:

> I had my lunch in the bathroom and someone walked in and he saw I didn't have any friends and he saw me at my most low, but never made fun of that. And I had some classes with him and he was nice to me and even invited me over at a football game. I had to stop caring about the impression I was making on people and had to break out of my shyness and I realized that I can't be seen like that again. I don't know what I was ashamed of, it was just big and loud and I didn't relate to people.

Students said that the non-Saint students at their private schools were not really mean, they just "were in their own worlds." Mari commented on how she just did not understand the conversations other students were having because they were so different from what she was used to talking about with her friends and family. But other students felt the lack of understanding more overtly. One student got in trouble for being late to homework club after spending time cleaning up a mess her group had made in her last class. She explained to her after-school teacher that she was late because

> we made a mess so we're cleaning it up. And [the teacher] said, "That's why we have janitors." I don't know, I feel like that is kind of a privileged thing to say. If I make a mess, I'm going to clean it up. At that point [in high school] I felt more comfortable hanging out with the janitors, but it just felt more like at home because I could speak Spanish with them and it's just very nice and they're very nice. I think also I had a deep respect for their work because that's what my parents are. I was like, I respect your profession and your role here in our school.

Some students pushed back against the lack of representation they saw in their private high schools. They saw the lack of diversity in their teachers and staff and asked why. They advocated for clubs to bring students together based on their ethnicity and to support one another. Although it took years, subsequent Saint alumni were able to continue to ask for clubs and eventually the school allowed their formation.

Because students felt that the chance to attend private school on scholarship was something they could not throw away, most found ways to get through each day. Like Anthony, Veronica dealt with her feelings of isolation by keeping to herself and doing her schoolwork and not much else while at school. Other students kept their friendships mainly to students from Saint. Familiarity with elite, mainly white schools and spaces and the resources embedded in these places can provide a cultural advantage for low-income students later when they encounter such spaces at elite colleges and workplaces (Jack 2016; 2019).

Some Saint students left and transferred to public high schools. Rachel said she thought of leaving St. Theresa often:

> Junior year was my hardest. It was a lot of academic stuff, emotional stuff, and I did want to leave. But I didn't tell my parents because they [would think],

really, a really good school and you want to leave? You know you're at a private school. You know you should take advantage of it, but there are people where they can't handle it because private schools are a lot to handle honestly. I didn't want to be there, I didn't like my friends at the time. I didn't feel like I fit in. But I was like, "Rachel suck it in." But I didn't tell anyone because I didn't want anyone judging me or anything. I sucked it up. We would all count down the days to graduation.

The students who attended schools with few Saint alumni had the most difficult time. Students who were involved in sports or other extracurricular activities usually did meet non-Saint students and considered them friends. However, there was little "hanging out after school" or going to these friends' houses. And non-Saint friends rarely went to their houses.

The assumption behind school choice and voucher models is that students and parents will have the freedom to choose the best schools and then get to experience the same outcomes available to upper-class families. But it does not work that way for low-income students. Some studies find that students from low-income neighborhoods who go to schools with white, wealthy students have worse outcomes than if they would have gone to a high school that better matched them demographically (Crosnoe 2009; Owens 2010). These are surprising findings given the number of programs that have been developed to try to enroll low-income students in schools with mainly high-income students. Crosnoe (2009) notes that the issue is one of equity in the integration of students, and as Lewis and Diamond (2015) demonstrated, even well-meaning administrators are not able to accomplish such integration without persistent work on the issues that restrict opportunities. The structural constraints embedded in racially and economically segregated high schools shape student experiences in ways that follow them to college, with students from highly ranked academic high schools usually being more comfortable in largely white environments but having trouble connecting with same-race peers who went to more racially diverse high schools (Torres and Massey 2012).

The current demographics in the Catholic secondary school system influenced Saint students and their experiences of race and class. Although Catholic schools have a history of educating new immigrants from Europe, most of whom came from low-income families, today Catholic high schools are dominated by students who come from white, wealthy backgrounds whose families immigrated to the United States many generations ago. Even though Catholic schools also attract students from low-income and middle-class families who are stretching the family budget to send their kids to a private school, the schools often "feel rich." This is particularly true in the California Bay Area, where the median household income is over $110,000. Catholic high school tuition is usually around $20,000 a year. By comparison, the most expensive private non-Catholic school in the area is $48,500 a year.

Most Saint families earned less than $30,000 annually. Yesenia described how differences in social class showed up at her Catholic school this way: "I did feel a little out of place sometimes, it wasn't easy for me to do this, to do that. Certain girls would want to go do this, go on a road trip, or let's do this. I can't do that you know? My dad gives me what he can and I'm grateful for that. I know I can't ask him for more. So, I started working so I wouldn't have to ask him. But there was that difference in terms of, you know, your family is well off, mine is, we're just getting by kind of things." She felt that was one reason why she stayed "within the same group of girls from Saint, cause that's where I felt most comfortable."

Given that many graduating eighth-graders at Saint attended private schools, talking about the demographic differences students would likely encounter in high school while they were still in middle school was very important. Staff knew that for Saint students to stay on the educational track it was imperative that they be able to adjust to the differences they would encounter in transitioning to high schools and that they not assume that they were "less than" the students from more wealthy families. Students felt their parents could not understand that they might have a difficult time attending very white private schools. Said one student, "Parents aren't prepared to understand their child when their child says, 'I don't fit in and I don't like this experience.'"

While some may assume that the culture shock that Saint students experienced at their private high schools can be mitigated by attending a high school more demographically similar to their middle school, that only delays facing the same feelings of "difference" when enrolling in college, especially those with the highest graduation rates. Many studies of racially underrepresented students adjusting to colleges with primarily white, European American student bodies find similar experiences of isolation and uncertainty about identity and place (Khan 2011; Lee 2005). Said Patty, who had attended a charter high school with similar demographics to Saint, about her first semester at college, "My seven roommates they were all white except for two and no Latinos. But they came from rich families and I could never really relate to them and it was hard because I didn't really have anyone who could understand my situation. I was always looking for scholarships. I felt like I didn't belong and I really wanted to quit, I felt like these girls have more money, they look like they are smarter than me. I don't think I belong here, and it took a really long time for me to be like, 'No, I can do this. I belong here.'"

A small number of Saint students who attended private high schools said that the demographic differences did not bother them and they did not hesitate to be involved on campus; others said that they found ways to "get through" high school so they could move on to better things for themselves. All were grateful for the opportunity that Saint provided in introducing them to different schools and helping them to be academically prepared as well as helping them to access financial aid options. Even so, students had to individually figure out how to feel comfortable in this new environment.

Parental Involvement and Fulfilling Family Needs

Saint Middle School prides itself on serving the whole family. Over the time of this study the school was continuing to find new ways to include parents in the everyday life of the school. Parents helped with fund-raising and special events on campus. Bilingual office staff and teachers also helped parents to feel welcomed and included. Workshops to inform parents about how they could help their students with homework and high school applications as well as individual meetings with families were key to this process. And parents were very responsive and attended these meetings.

But when Saint students went to high school, this dynamic changed, especially at the private schools where most teachers, school administrators, and other parents did not speak Spanish. And the public schools were so large that reaching administration and teachers was difficult. Students were "on their own." The lessened involvement of parents, especially at the private high schools, is particularly disconcerting given research demonstrating that parental involvement in high school is especially important in predicting postsecondary education for students from more disadvantaged backgrounds (Benner, Boyle, and Sadler 2016).

In contrast, the charter high school was much more parent friendly, with many staff who spoke Spanish. It was also small and, like Saint, community oriented. The school recognized the importance of bringing in parents and did so particularly around college application time, including holding workshops to inform parents about the process, steps, and forms required to apply for federal and state financial aid.

The reduced ability of parents to be involved in their children's' high schools combined with a lessened understanding by high school staff about the family situations of students made transitioning to the demands of high school (and later college) particularly challenging for students who also needed to help their families. These duties usually increased over their time in high school. Students often were strong academically and on the college track, but they also had many family responsibilities. For some it was the need to help care for younger siblings, especially after they could drive. In Yesenia's case, the increased responsibilities started sophomore year of high school after the birth of her brother. Her mom owned her own business and had to go back to work, and she relied on Yesenia to go home immediately after school to take care of her brother. As a result, she became very attached to him, which influenced her later decision to go to college where she could live at home.

For other students it was the need to support themselves and contribute to the family income that influenced their experiences in high school and subsequently their college options post–high school. As mentioned at the beginning of this chapter, Veronica worked throughout high school to help support her immediate family and also to send money to extended family in Mexico. But when she became estranged from her family she needed money to support herself with housing, food, and other basic necessities. Friends, rather than teachers, were greater sources of support and understanding to help her find jobs and ultimately obtain a full-time job she loved.

Preparing for the Next Transition: College Advising and Asking for Help

For students from high-income families, the college application process is often a time that parents get more involved in their students' high school experience, helping them find and visit potential colleges, meet with high school counselors, ask others to help with the application process, and guide them in making acceptance decisions as well as paying the bills associated with applying and enrolling in college (Holland 2019; Lareau, Evans, and

Yee 2016; McDonough 1997). But the parents of potential first-generation college students often step back even more than they did during the transition to high school. And although students in the United States have heard about attending college since kindergarten, high school is the time that the idea of attending college becomes real. Obtaining good grades, participating in activities, visiting colleges, and researching college options all become important on the path to attending college right after high school. In high school opportunities for participation in clubs and sports grow, and students often decide what to participate in based on what "will look good on my college application." High school is also the time when grades matter; AP and honors courses are seen as goods valued by colleges, and students take the ACT or SAT (or not). Students also decide during this time which schools to apply to determined partially on how they assess their progress on the list of what matters to colleges.

Studies have found that the strategies that high schools employ to help students apply to college matter, and not surprisingly, schools with fewer resources are less successful than those with more (Klugman 2012). Hill (2008) found that high schools that provided a variety of supports, including assisting with admission and financial aid applications, involving parents, and contacting college representatives, were "brokering" schools. Schools that provided such resources had higher rates of students enrolling in college than did schools that offered some but not all of these supports.

As shown in the analysis of national data presented in chapter 1, a very high percentage of first-generation and continuing-generation students said they had met with a college counselor by their junior year of high school. This is important because being a potential first-generation college student usually means relying heavily on college counselors for help (Fallon 1997). College counselors help with the college application process, keep students aware of the strict deadlines, and show students how to tell the difference between types of schools, majors, costs, and other factors not easy to understand, especially for anyone not familiar with the U.S. education system. Yet the high schools with the most students who need intensive college counseling have few counselors. In 2009–2010 there was one counselor for every 810 students in California public high schools (Frey 2012). The American School Counselor Association recommends a ratio of one counselor for every 250 students. Saint students at public high schools usually met with a counselor once or not at all.

Researching Colleges

Saint students who attended private schools said that their high school teachers and advisors started talking about college during their sophomore year, with more intensive advising throughout the junior year. Students were instructed to research schools using an online program, and the school sponsored visits by admissions officers, held college nights, and organized trips to colleges in the state. Some students learned about programs that would pay for them to visit schools on the East Coast. Most of the students visited schools before they applied.

College counselors promoted the idea that students should apply to a number of different types of schools, including private colleges that students defined as expensive. Students became excited about the potential opportunity to attend such schools, especially after visiting. College counselors also helped them with their financial aid applications, although it appeared that a counselor's knowledge of financial aid processes varied substantially, even between those in the same school. The students with counselors they felt could not help them figured out the financial aid forms on their own, or went back to Saint and got help from the director of graduate support or the principal. Said Jeanne about why she did not go to her high school counselor for help with college applications, "No, I didn't talk to the [high school] counselors, I was more leaning on the [principal at Saint] just because I felt a lot more comfortable talking to him, not that the counselors I had at school weren't, it's just that I've known him for years and I would go back [to Saint] a lot."

I asked Veronica what would have made it easier to ask for help from a high school teacher and advisor when she was struggling her last year of high school. She said, "Saint did a great job in that they showed me what it was to be a teacher, the teachers sacrificed, they put out their own money to buy books and other things, they knew that we struggled. I feel that more schools should be like Saint. They took care of us and showed us a whole new world that most of us didn't even know that they existed, all these different schools, opportunities." What Veronica needed from her high school was someone who comprehended her situation and could affirm her struggles. That could have opened the door for her to reach out for help.

Practically speaking, sometimes the high school counselors at private schools were not familiar with how to fill out federal and state financial aid forms, especially if parents or the students and their parents were undocumented. Two students, including Isabel, whose parents are undocumented had financial aid forms that were not processed when trying to submit additional information, and they forgot they had to mail in their parents' signature page again.[2] This was something high school counselors did not always understand and students did not necessarily expect them to know.

Choosing Which College

In choosing which colleges to apply to and attend, Ali, whom we will learn more about in the next chapter, had other ideas than her counselor, who pushed her to focus on state schools in California:

> One of the things I remember not liking about my college counselor, I get that she was being practical because she knew which students were coming from the backgrounds that we're coming from and they very much pushed the state schools in California just for the financial aid to make it more financially feasible, but I figured that you're working this hard you should be able to have more options even though I did understand the financial part of it. . . . I saved money because I was working and I wanted to visit two of the schools [out of state] where I applied and was accepted. My oldest sister flew out with me and I loved one of them and ended up going there.

High school teachers who shared where they went to college were influential in the college choice process, as were teachers who would give students a "backstage" tour during campus visits. Joseph, who went to College Prep Charter, became excited about doing well in high school after his teachers took him and his classmates on college visits and he could see the schools where his teachers went.

Students who attended private schools and did not get into the colleges they applied to or who decided to attend the local state school or community college usually did not go back and tell their high school counselors. They said they made the decision on their own after considering the costs. They knew that students at their school attended "prestigious" colleges and thought counselors would be disappointed in their choices.

Similarly, Isabel did not tell her high school counselor when her federal financial aid forms did not go through because she forgot to mail in her parents' form. She was in her second year of attending community college and hoped to transfer to a four-year school, however she had not yet started the application process and did not know who to go to for help. And because his high school counselor encouraged him to, Alex applied to four-year schools that would require him to move away from home, even though he knew all along he would attend the local state college and continue to live with his mom.

Samuel did not get into any of the schools to which he applied. Then he wanted to attend a state college about forty minutes away, but his parents said he was not mature enough to live away from home. He never went back to talk to his high school advisor about other options. Ricky had good support from his counselor to determine which schools to apply to, and he "made it my job to go see him," but he was disappointed that his counselor did not tell him that his SAT score might limit the financial aid he got from schools, forcing him to attend the cheaper state school when he really wanted to go to a private college like his high school: "I feel like he could have told me a lot more, especially with the testing prep or he could have emphasized that more because I didn't really have the resources that students have because they signed up for classes, for tutors to help them out. That's something I noticed that was a privilege I was not aware of before."

Veronica was in a different situation: "I really wanted to go to college, but there was not enough money." Because she was estranged from her parents she could not get the necessary information from them, and they were undocumented, which added steps to the financial aid process: "My senior year was when I started living on my own and I couldn't get any information from my parents. At the end of the day I still needed to do my homework, find a place to sleep, find a place to shower. Most people at my school didn't have to struggle like I had to. Most of the things people took for granted they shouldn't. We take a lot for granted. A lot of people don't have a place to sleep or food, clothes. I know what that is like."

High schools do not have staff who check back in with their graduates once they receive their diplomas. Students are presumed to be fine as they are handed off to the next level of education. However, for Saint students, especially those living in families vulnerable because of poverty and health issues, a lot could have happened to change their plans after college admission decisions came out.

Conclusion

For the students I spoke with, high school became a time of either growing or diminishing opportunities for their future. While students felt able to do the academic work asked of them, those who fell off the college track usually experienced some form of disruption while in high school. One student worked instead of focusing on school, another had to move three hundred miles away very suddenly because of family issues, another struggled with depression. They rarely let anyone at their high schools know "what was really going on."

The students interviewed for this project did well academically. They had shown promise on entrance exams before middle school and were presented with a rigorous middle school curriculum that challenged them and prepared them well for the most academically recognized high schools in the area. As a result, the academic transition from middle to high school was relatively easy; in fact, when students attended public schools the transition was "too easy" and they often did the minimal work required of them.

At the high school level students who stayed on the college track benefited from being able to return to their middle school for homework and other support while they were transitioning to their new school; a required college preparatory curriculum; intensive advising, especially during their junior year when preparing to take the SAT/ACT; other students and teachers who understood them; and student clubs that celebrated their ethnicities and identities. The students who stayed on the traditional college path usually had a very involved high school counselor combined with family economic stability.

Following students' educational trajectories show how the instability that comes with poverty derailed some students. Students never told their advisors, teachers, or anyone at their high schools about why their grades were slipping or the reasons they were unable to complete financial aid and college enrollment forms. Poverty also meant that many high-achieving students needed to work instead of focusing on school, delay or change college plans, choose the closest and cheapest college option, and, in a few cases, focus more on everyday survival over academic advancement. And those students who applied to but did not get into private high schools then attended other schools with very low college placement and found themselves on paths that no longer led to college.

In terms of what this chapter contributes to debates about school choice, as private schools and charter schools do not often have to report the same kinds of data as traditional public schools, parents and students are not able to easily compare schools. And districts are limited in what they can do to collect these data. This also causes problems for middle school principals and teachers who are often asked by parents what high schools they would recommend but they do not know how their students do as they move on to a wide variety of high schools.

Although Saint graduated students in eighth grade with the academic potential to do well in high school, the type of high school they attended influenced their path to college. In the next chapter we will learn more about the five main paths that Saint alumni took as they graduated from high school. We will see how a variety of factors influenced the path that they took and will learn more about the experiences of Samuel, Isabel, Alex, Veronica, and Ali as they attempted to be the first in their families to attend and graduate from college.

4

College Transitions

———————————————————●

Five Paths Post–High School

> I really, really wanted to go away to
> college. Live in a big city. Go to a small,
> private college. Everyone in my family
> told me to stop dreaming so much. But
> I was determined to make it work and,
> with the help of those who wanted to
> share my journey, I did.
> —Ali

Ali applied to sixteen colleges. The application, decision, and first year of
college were full of worry and struggle: figuring out which schools to apply
to and how to complete the financial aid forms; deciphering the financial
aid awards and which offers made the most sense; convincing her parents
that spending so much money on going away to school was worth it; finding jobs and paying for living expenses the first year; and then, at the end of
the year, convincing her parents again that going away for school was still
worth it, even though her parents could no longer help financially. They tried
to convince her that living at home would be so much cheaper. And being

away was creating additional strain for her family, who depended on Ali to help translate at medical appointments for her parents and younger sister.

All Saint alumni understood that the ideal educational trajectory was to enroll in a four-year college right after finishing high school. And the idea of moving away from home and having a fun and independent experience being a full-time college student was appealing to many Saint alum. But Ali's experience highlights typical issues that occur for first-generation students when they attempt to take this traditional path to college, which was challenging even for those students with the highest grades and who went to high schools where most of their classmates were on the same path.

The rest of this chapter describes the five different paths to college that first-generation students from Saint took. These paths provide clues for high schools, colleges, and policy makers about what needs to change to increase the college completion rates of first-generation college students. In chapter 5 I will summarize the common issues that students faced from middle school to college.

Differential Paths in the Transition Post–High School

The five different paths that Saint alumni took after finishing high school and as young adults were the following: Ali's traditional college path; Alex's hybrid traditional path; Isabel's working student path; Samuel's meandering path; and Veronica's work/family path. Studying each path provides insights into what issues get students offtrack when working toward a college degree and provides an opportunity to understand the factors that cut across different experiences as well as the potential interventions necessary to raise the college completion rates of first-generation college students.

Table 4.1 shows the paths post–high school of all Saint alumni who graduated eighth grade the same years as did those interviewed. Thirty percent were on the traditional path of attending a four-year school away from home. Students who had attended a Catholic, private high school were the most likely to be on that path. Of alumni, 17 percent were on the hybrid traditional path, attending a four-year school and living at home. A quarter were attending a two-year community college and working. And then about 10 percent of students had attended multiple colleges without receiving a degree or certification. Finally, 18 percent of students had not attended college after graduating from high school or attended a very short time and

Table 4.1
Paths Post–High School for Interviewees and Full Population of Saint Alumni, by High School Type

Paths Post–High School	Interviewees (n = 42)	Full Population of Saint Alumni (N = 154)	Went to Private HS (n = 79)	Went to Public HS (n = 75)
Traditional college (%)	36	30	51	8
Hybrid traditional (%)	19	17	23	11
Working student (%)	17	25	14	39
Meandering/dead end (%)	19	10	10	9
Work/family (%)	10	18	3	33

dropped out. Instead they were working and/or taking care of children or other family members.

As the table shows, there was a lower proportion of students interviewed who were on the working student and work/family paths (e.g., while 18 percent of all Saint alumni were on the work/family path, only 10 percent of the interviewees were). Students on the work/family path were the most difficult to schedule interviews with. Their work shifts changed often, and included night shifts, and they had few days or predictable time off. Therefore, a limitation of this study is not talking to more students on the work/family path.

For those who attended college, in table 4.2, we see that the characteristics of the colleges differed considerably, including their graduation rates. Ali attended a school with the highest graduation rate, and she was one of the few Saint alumni who completed her degree in four years. Samuel, now on the meandering path, had started at Local State U, where Alex is in his fifth year. Local State U has a 40 percent six-year graduation rate for Latina/o students. But Samuel was disenrolled from the school and now attends a two-year community college with one of the lowest graduation rates: a 16 percent three-year graduation rate for Latina/o students and a 22 percent rate of graduation for all students.

Traditional College Path

About a third of all Saint alumni who graduated eighth grade took the traditional path to college, enrolling in a four-year school away from home right after graduating from high school. Just over half of the students who

Table 4.2
Characteristics of Colleges Profiled Students Attended[a]

Student and Path	College Type	# Undergrad Students	% Pell	% Latina/o	% White	% First Gen	% 6-Year Grad All Students[a]	% 6-Year Grad Latina/o Students[a]
Ali—traditional	4-year private	10,168	27	14	58	27	71	60
Alex—hybrid traditional	4-year public	25,862	42	26	19	50	48	40
Isabel—working student	2-year public	9,636	15	27	44	46	28	24
Samuel—meandering	2-year public	9,446	22	44	17	58	22	16

SOURCE: Data from the Data Clearinghouse for the 2015–2016 academic year.

[a] For four-year schools, graduation rates are based on students who graduated in six years or less; for two-year schools, rates are based on students who graduated in three years or less. https://collegecompletion.chronicle.com.

graduated from a Catholic high school were on this path. Only 8 percent of Saint alumni who had attended a public or charter high school took the traditional path. While the traditional path was the one most encouraged by high schools, it was not a smooth transition for most first-generation college students.

Ali's experiences reveal the main issues for first-generation college students who are also low-income and whose family circumstances and backgrounds are not well represented at the private college she attended. We know that Ali put herself in the best position to finish a bachelor's degree by entering a four-year college with a good graduation rate directly after finishing high school and attending full-time. This is the path that most continuing-generation students, like Sarah, whom we met in chapter 1, take. A first-generation student who tries to follow this traditional path to college faces a number of obstacles that students whose parents have a college background and financial resources do not.

To take the traditional path to college, Ali had to get used to being in spaces where people were different from herself; she had to ignore comments from others that her dreams were "too high," figure out the mechanics of college such as course choice and financial aid on her own, and take out substantial loans. She also had to make sure she was pursuing a degree that made economic sense to her parents and manage the guilt she felt for not being available to provide more financially or translate regularly for her family. Ali said that her parents were always very supportive of her and her siblings getting a bachelor's degree, as "that's why they came to this country," but that they were not supportive of her going away to college. Ali believes she was able to do the traditional path because she found people who "wanted to share my journey" and helped support her emotionally in making choices that put her needs equal to the needs and wants of her family. She was also able to live with those who were supporting her college path, which allowed her to afford to attend college away from home and also to have some time to participate in activities at school. Of course she did work a lot while in college, but she did not have to drop out of school as some other graduates of Saint did.

Specifically, the transition to college was especially challenging for Ali for three main reasons: First, she needed more support than she received to determine her major. She came to college thinking she wanted to be a science major because she had been told that a career in science or as a lawyer was the best way to have a well-paying job. But college chemistry was academically challenging and she lost interest in the sciences. She was not sure how to go about figuring out what else she might be interested in and then how to change her major. She wanted to make sure she was doing something "practical and where I could get a good job right after graduating," but by the time she figured out science was not going to work out, it was too late to declare her second choice major—accounting—and graduate in four years. She chose a major she liked well enough, but most importantly that she could still finish in four years (which she had promised her parents was the main reason it was worth it to pay for a private college instead of a public college, where it would take more than four years to graduate). Poor support around academic planning almost derailed her aspirations for a bachelor's degree and the traditional college-going experience.

The second issue was the cost of college. Ali received scholarships that covered all of her tuition. But her parents needed to pay for housing and other expenses. It was too much. Even with Ali working numerous jobs during the first year, which got in the way of her being able to focus more on her science major and also was a source of stress, living expenses were too much for her parents. After the first year they told her they could not help her financially anymore, so she had to transfer to a school to which she could commute from home. Ali almost dropped out. But she shared her problems with a family who had just moved to town and were friends with her high school sponsor. Their youngest child was going away to college, and they offered her room to Ali. Beyond providing housing, they also supported Ali and encouraged her to live out her dreams, to be involved at school, and to not work too much. She did get more involved in college when she could, but she still worked full-time in a variety of jobs her whole time in college. She would work before classes, starting at five thirty in the morning, and then go to a different job after classes ended and add as many hours as she could on the weekends. She lived with this family for two years and was able to save enough money to pay for her own shared apartment her senior year. Although her first priority was being a student, she was not able to have the traditional college experience that she wanted and saw other students having.

The third factor that made the transition to college difficult was overcoming guilt for not being at home to help her family more. Ali was the main translator for her Spanish-speaking parents, and because her younger sibling had medical issues, her parents needed her to help translate at medical appointments. Ali's older sister and mother would call her and tell her she needed to come home to help. Ali wavered between believing the family she lived with saying it was okay for her to pursue her own dreams, assuring her that she was not being selfish by not complying with all the requests from her family.

Ali graduated college in four years and is now in a master's program in business. She receives free housing as a full-time nanny and takes classes at night. She credits her parents as being the most important force in her completing college: "It really is difficult leaving the [poverty] cycle. I was lucky my parents knew education was the only way to leave that cycle. That's a big reason why I went to college, my mom didn't finish ninth grade and my dad stopped in middle school. My parents always said they wanted us, their children, 'to be better than us.' They always said, 'That is why we came to this country.'" Ali still helps her parents from afar, filling out financial aid forms for her younger sister, calling people for her parents when they need help, and sending money home to help pay bills.

For Elise, it was her high school counselor whom she credited with helping her apply to and ultimately enroll at UC: "She was definitely a big motivator. I'm the first one to ever go to college in my family so I didn't know what the journey was, what the process is like. Things like 'make sure to sign up for Saturday to take your SATs.' So, I can definitely thank my high school counselor for guiding me through that whole process and she's the reason why I applied to the school I did and why I am in college right now." When visiting UC the first time, Elise said, "I absolutely fell in love with the school. I mean, I saw that all the faces around me were predominately white, but that was no longer a struggle for me because that was the same as my high school. I think that's what helped me to transition to this university a lot quicker than other of my classmates who have gone to school only with other Latinos their whole lives. And I didn't feel the exclusion that they did coming in." What also helped was telling herself that it was okay for her to focus on school now: "For so long I had been doing everything for my family and I thought of it this way, these four years I may be away from home, but it will serve as a foundation for me to provide my family with a better future. So, in some part I was doing it for me, but also I would help my family at the end of the day." Elise also was able to share her experience of getting into and going to college with her family:

UC has receptions for their top applicants, but [at the reception] they told us we had all been admitted. I went with my mom. It was the first university I was accepted to, and I experienced it with my mom. And it was so great. I felt so recognized for all the hard work. It was a beautiful experience for me, and I was the only one [in my family] who was thinking something bigger for college, so it was a very rewarding experience. And that made me say, "This is where I want to go." At first my mom tried to convince me that it was too far, but then she saw how committed I was and she was supportive.

Like Ali, living on campus the first year was the most financially challenging part of being on the traditional path. Once she moved off campus and worked more hours, Elise was able to finish college in four years with no loans: "I am very good with money. Financially I have really struggled. I have been literally broke twice, but my mom has been there and I've never taken advantage of it. I only ask her for help with my tuition. My mom came from Mexico with nothing, has raised four kids on her own, and went from being someone's worker to being her own boss. She is my motivation right now, and we are financially stable because of her owning her own business."

Most students had taken out loans, usually to pay for living experiences. Taking out loans and not telling their parents was a common strategy that Saint alumni took to stay on the traditional path to college. Said Martha, "I didn't tell my parents at first because I knew their reaction would be like 'we would pay,' but I feel bad, I still feel bad that I'm going to college because my mom works, basically three jobs and my dad is a driver and I feel bad that I'm going to a school that is 60K a year." Being a resident assistant helped Martha pay for living expenses her third year in college.

Ali had almost $75,000 in loans by the time she graduated and continued to take out loans for graduate school. The three Saint students on the traditional path who did not take out any loans had very generous scholarships that covered tuition, room, board, fees, books, and other living expenses. The scholarships also adjusted each year as tuition was raised. These students lived on campus, and the one of the three with the most generous national scholarship did not work while taking classes. He concentrated on school, came home only for winter break and some summers, and was provided academic, emotional, and social support from the scholarship program. He was on track to graduate in four years and then apply to medical school.

Students on the traditional path lived on campus their first year and, if not out of state, often came home most every weekend. These students all said that they learned early on that it was better for them to not go home so much and instead work and send money home when they could. Students still helped their parents and younger siblings with paperwork related to their own schooling. Some talked to their parents every day about how things were going and made phone calls for them when they needed help with medical issues, insurance, younger siblings' schooling, and so forth. Students whose families were the most economically and emotionally stable were the most likely to be able to stay on the traditional path.

The academic adjustment to college was not difficult for students on the traditional path, but the social adjustment was challenging for some. Programs such as the Equal Opportunity Program (EOP) for first-generation students were helpful to many students, mainly by making the social transition easier. Said Elise about the EOP,

> Over the summer they have a weeklong transition program in which we attended classes and get a feel of the campus. So, I came in with no friends and made a lot of friends through that program and we all lived in the same residence hall the first quarter. Emotionally that was the hardest transition for me because I am extremely family oriented and I had never left my house for an extensive period of time. And I was the main mediator for my younger brother . . . and I helped take care of my younger sister since she was born so I have a very developed bond with her. When you first leave for college you are so excited, "I'm going to have so much fun, this year will be great." But then as time progressed I was homesick and I used ride shares to go home extensively during my first year. Sometimes three weekends in a month.

Getting more involved in clubs on campus and getting a job her second year reduced the visits Elise made to home.

Hybrid Traditional Path

Close to 20 percent of Saint alumni took the hybrid traditional path to college, attending a four-year school while also living at home. All the students who followed the hybrid traditional path post–high school attended high schools that promoted the traditional college path for their graduates. However, students altered the path by taking the most financially feasible option of attending the local state school while also living at home.

Students on the hybrid path all received enough federal and state aid (or DREAM scholarships if they were undocumented) to cover their tuition and were able to work as well as help with the needs of their families. These students were academically strong, many graduated from private high schools, and they were very motivated to complete their bachelor's degree.

Alex, whom we met in chapter 2, took the hybrid traditional path. Although he was accepted at UC and a number of other colleges, he always knew that the local state school, referred to as Local State U, which he could attend while living with his single mom, would be the cheapest choice. A business major, Alex followed the same motto of school first, work second, that he did in high school. On breaks and some weekends he worked, as he had in high school, with his mom at her bakery job. Alex credited his mom with always emphasizing school and making sure he applied to Saint and then Cardinal High School.

To stay on the path to a four-year degree, hybrid traditional students had to go off the traditional path by working off campus and continuing to help family. But the financial support, relative economic stability of their families, and ability to live at home with those who supported them in continuing to put school first allowed them to focus on school. They continued the discipline they learned in middle school of prioritizing academics. They also learned how to navigate a big college, taking early morning classes that usually did not overenroll, and finding good advisors and mentors. These students typically did not return to their high schools to check in with counselors, but sometimes they volunteered to tutor at their middle school. A cousin or significant other who also attended Local State U was an additional good source of support for some students.

Yesenia's high school teachers were key to getting her onto the hybrid path. Initially her teachers were encouraging her to move away and go to a private college in California, but when that would have required her to take out loans, Yesenia chose to go to Local State U. She said about her high school teacher who had taken her to visit colleges, "She supported me and she also told me that if I ever went back [to my high school] I could guide students who were in the same position, like first-generation. Cause when you're first-generation you don't really have your family in terms of support or like, what do I do? What classes do I take? So, for me it was a lot of help from mentors, like teachers, that guided me through that." While applying to colleges Yesenia also returned to Saint with her parents to attend workshops about filling out FAFSA financial aid forms. Even though Yesenia received a lot of support, her transition to Local State U was not easy. Her financial aid package was incorrect multiple times, interfering with her ability to register for courses on time and creating extra stress at the beginning of two semesters.

For other high-achieving students, their experience in high school was mirrored on the hybrid college path. In high school these students worked hard to keep up their grades, complete their hours for their high school scholarship, and work outside jobs. Similarly, their college choices were constricted by money and the need to work to contribute to rent for the whole family. Students felt they were making the "smart choice" by attending the four-year state school in their home city, and continuing to live at home and help with family. The graduate support director at Saint sighed when talking about this group of students. She said that many did or could have easily gotten into a UC school, with higher graduation rates and more prestige, and that students would have qualified for ample financial aid to attend. But they would have had to live away from home to attend, something that students who felt they had a lot of family responsibilities were loath to do.

The students who took the hybrid traditional path would likely be classified as having undermatched their academic abilities to the selectivity of the school they attended (Dillon and Smith 2017; Howell and Pender 2015; Ovink et al. 2018). Their grades, standardized test scores, and extracurricular activities resulted in them being accepted to a number of more selective schools with higher graduation rates than Local State U. But these students looked at the financial aid awards and considered the living expenses, and decided that the smartest path would be to live at home. In addition, in the case of many students, their parents needed their financial help to pay the rent and/or other living expenses. The cost of maintaining two separate living spaces made no sense to them. Sofía, who had a 3.7 GPA at her rigorous private high school, got into all the colleges she applied to except Stanford. She did not really want to go to Local State U and live at home, but

they would just send those big envelopes with all the brochures and everything and then in there is your financial aid packet. I remember one state school in [the Midwest] was the one that I really wanted to go to, if I had a preference, that was it. But they only gave me like $5,000 and it's like $48,000 and I was like nope, good-bye. So, then the two highest ones were—the first packet that I got—I was like, this might be manageable, I think was somewhere in Washington. It was a private school and I got the dean's scholarship, but I still had to take out like a—there's a possibility that I still had to take out a loan and I was—and I did the math, I was like if I don't take out the loan how much do I have to pay and how much do I have to work? That's really difficult. And then I finally got [the package from] Local State U and they were like you get more than tuition, so, I was like, okay.

Those on the hybrid path worked at a variety of retail jobs and also were adding on internships to help strengthen their experience. But those on the hybrid path had to be careful not to work too much. Because most were working off-campus jobs, at places where they had started working while in high school, their responsibilities increased over time. Anthony was put on academic probation after his first semester at Local State U because he did not complete enough units. He was working, almost full-time, in security at night and taking classes during the day. The spring semester he cut his hours and was off probation by his second year. While work was still a big part of his life, he was fully committed to his major in economics and hoped to eventually work in business.

Like the students attending public colleges on the traditional path, students on the hybrid path also benefited from being part of the EOP at Local State U. The program provided extra advising resources, money for books, and help with course registration. Joining campus clubs related to their majors also served as a way to meet other students and have access to more on-campus mentors.

Students on the hybrid path continued to live with their families, usually in the neighborhoods where they grew up near Saint. Most families rented. Even though gentrification is beginning to affect the neighborhood near Saint, the students said that their families had good relationships with their landlords and they could handle the rent increases each year as they were able to work more and help with the rent. But Saint alumni experienced the neighborhood differently as they became older. Rachel liked living where she knew everyone, but was getting tired of all the harassing comments she got from men hanging out on the street while she was walking to her car. Anthony mentioned being nervous when guys would walk up to him, especially when he was dating someone new. Regina, whose family moved out of the Saint neighborhood but came back to visit her old neighbors, said, "When I lived here I was never scared, because I was just used to it, but I come back now [to visit] and I'm kind of scared. I don't know why. It's kind of scary at night and you see some gangsters or whatever. So, for me now it's just kind of scary." Staying local also allowed students on the hybrid path to help siblings, cousins, and younger alumni from Saint to navigate the college path.

Working Student Path

In contrast to students on the hybrid and traditional paths, students on the working student path devoted similar amounts of time and energy to working and being a student. Almost all the students in this group attended community college directly after high school and lived at home with their parents. They graduated from a variety of types of high schools (public, charter, and private). Their reasons for not attending a four-year school directly after high school were varied but mainly centered around problems with financial aid applications during the college application process as well as circumstances during high school such as depression or missing school for health or family reasons that impeded their ability to apply to college during the fall of their senior year of high school. All of the students in this group completed high school and aspired to obtain a bachelor's degree. But the real need for money now pulled them to find ways to balance working and going to school.

We first met Isabel at the start of chapter 1. She applied to and was accepted to a mix of private and public colleges, but her financial aid forms were not fully processed when she forgot to mail in a form after making a change online because her mom was undocumented. Her mom's situation had caused her to have to move to two different schools in one semester while in high school, but she was still able to graduate from St. Theresa high school with good grades. But Isabel was overwhelmed by all the steps required to apply to college along with her other responsibilities during her last two years in high school.

Because of the need to help drive her younger siblings to school, Isabel could not attend college sessions held early in the mornings at high school and she was not clear about the different financial aid options: "Yeah, I'm the first in my family to go to college and we didn't have any idea what we were doing, and they were giving us information, they told us things and they tried to keep us up to date and everything but it's so much information." Needing to mail in some of her FAFSA application also made meeting all the deadlines difficult: "And like on the financial aid, I made a correction on the FAFSA and I forgot to send in the signature again, and I kept on contacting them over and over, and I guess they didn't know the signature was missing and they kinda didn't give me the correct information I needed so by the time I realized that's what the issue was, it was kinda late. In the FAFSA, you can sign the signature online only if your parent has a social security. Otherwise you have to mail it in."

Isabel relied more on the graduate support director at Saint rather than counselors at her high school to make decisions about college. Saint staff helped her through all of her school transitions. Although Isabel said that her high school counselor was very helpful, she just did not have time to meet with her. Once starting at the local community college, the graduate support director at Saint helped Isabel get into the EOP. Besides extra advising support, EOP at her community college also provided visits to four-year colleges and resources to help with transferring to a four-year college.

Like for Isabel, financial aid issues because of an undocumented parent also affected Lizbeth, who had to drop out of community college for a year to work full-time when her mom had to leave the country unexpectedly. Lizbeth stopped school to contribute more to the family income. She is back at her community college now and found a job that is more flexible with her school schedule.

The types of jobs that students had were very important in their being able to equally prioritize school and work. Isabel had one of the best jobs of the working students because an internship she found in high school had expanded and was flexible enough for her to stay consistently enrolled in the local community college. "I started off as a high school intern and they moved me up to a college intern and you actually get paid a little more. So, it's been great, they trust me with different projects now, and when they have new interns, I'm the one who kinda goes around and helps them with their own work too. Yeah definitely they've helped me become more independent, I guess I wasn't much of a leader, but it has helped me learn how to be a little more in charge of things." The internship also has provided enough financial stability to help her family and still allows her to help her mom on the weekends with her job painting houses:

> Cause I help my mom, and I know the work now too so we go much faster now with two people who know how to do the job. And also with my internship, I pay most of my own expenses except for rent and food. Yeah, but everything else, I pay for my own expenses, and I help pay for some of my sibling's expenses too. So, financially it's gotten much, much better now . . . and my internship, they're really great, because I'm taking a break for the summer because I have too many classes, but they've been like, "Oh, once you're done with classes, just come back whenever. And you'll keep working on your projects and everything."

Rachel also had a job that was flexible with school: "I asked my mangers if my schedule will interfere with school and he said that no, they would arrange around it. With my school schedule and everything they're pretty good about like if I say I can't that day, or I have school in the mornings they won't force me to go in or anything. So they are really flexible."

Students on the working student path were very dependent on workplaces that supported the flexibility they needed to go to school with changing schedules each semester. But if their jobs required them to work more or during school times, and given the immediate need for financial resources for not only themselves but also their families, students were at risk of dropping out of school if they needed to keep their jobs.

For students who were both working and going to school, their futures were less certain than those of the students who followed the traditional and hybrid paths to college. When asked about her future plans, Isabel said, "Right now, I really don't know. A year ago, in high school I would have been, 'Oh, I'm gonna go to this college and I'm going to study this.' But now, I'm gonna go with the flow and see where I end up. . . . Hopefully something [at my internship] will work out for a job."

Marta was the only Saint alumnus on the working student path who started at a four-year school, but was trying to go to a two-year school after facing financial troubles at Local State U that prevented her from registering for courses. She was working full-time as a server while also studying full-time. She was upset that her private high school never talked about two-year schools, which she felt would have been a much better first choice for her:

I do feel that private [high] schools, because of reputation, really push students to only consider four-year colleges, which for me didn't work out. So yeah, I was kind of annoyed. . . . I feel like a lot of schools are really trying to get that percentage of four-year college-goers, but for some people, especially if you don't have enough money and financial aid, it's just such a pain to worry about those first few years. And you need to know what to major in because every school is so impacted and you need to get into [your major] really, really quickly because there is a lot of competition around you to even get the classes that you want and you have to get the prereqs and then apply to the major you want. And at four-year colleges you're more time-limited. You can't just take a class for fun because that cost like a thousand dollars and at community colleges it's a lot more affordable. I mean, if you have the money then I guess it doesn't matter. . . . The students that go to my high school, their parents are really educated and stuff like that. So going to a two-year is viewed as bad and that you're not succeeding. If they changed the way they perceived two-year schools or the way they showed them to be, it would help students not feel as embarrassed to see if they want to go to a two-year school.

Students on the working student path understood the difficulty of trying to equally balance school and work. Marta was considering stopping school for some time: "I might not take classes next semester and save up some money so that I can comfortably go to class and not work as much during the whole semester." Students who had more financial stressors or jobs that were not flexible were the most at risk of quitting school or stopping school intermediately, which was the experience of students on the next path.

Dead Ends and Meandering through Multiple Colleges

Students on the meandering or dead-end path attended multiple postsec-ondary schools after graduating from high school, sometimes three or more colleges. About 10 percent of all Saint alumni were on this path. And about half of the students in this group had attended a private high school. Some students in this group started at a four-year school but then switched to one or more community colleges. Others attended multiple community colleges.

Attending multiple schools that led to few credits and a lack of scholarly direction was the experience of Samuel, whom we met in the introduction. Samuel attended a Catholic private high school where he struggled with his grades off and on. He said that Saint prepared him well academically, but his interests changed a lot during high school and he had troubling focus-ing. He connected with his high school science teacher who introduced him to marine biology, which he thought would be a great career. He also got very interested in playing football and wrestling, and he focused more on those things than on school. After his second year he was unable to stay on the teams because of his grades.

Samuel graduated high school in four years and applied to four-year col-leges, but the only school he was accepted to was a state school about forty miles away. His parents told him he was too young to move away to school. He eventually attended a small private school that became a for-profit dur-ing his time there. His family paid the tuition until he was able to be part of a special STEM program that covered his tuition. After the school closed they helped him transfer to the local state college. He continued to try to major in the sciences but could not pass chemistry. He was disenrolled from Local State U because of his grades and incomplete units. He then enrolled in a local community college, but still could not pass chemistry and his other required science courses. He transferred to a different community college, where he is taking engineering courses and delaying trying chemistry again. He found out about the STEM Club "out of luck. I was walking down a pathway, I saw like the billboard, so I went to it and signed up. I met with the director. They're like, all right, cool. And I started taking classes that were STEM core and those have been some of the best classes I've taken." He did well this semester. During all this he worked full-time, sometimes all night, at two different grocery stores. His plan is to work full-time in the summers and eventually to transfer back to Local State U.

Students like Samuel, who found themselves on a meandering path post–high school, attended multiple colleges and programs in an attempt to continue their educations. Most of the students taking this path also worked at a variety of jobs and were uncertain about where their schooling was leading them. Samuel had no idea what an associate's degree was until his girlfriend told him that he could get one at his current community college. This was a common issue among students who had attended a private high school and then enrolled in a two-year school. Xochi said she wished that her high school had at least talked about community college as an option, instead of assuming that the only option was to attend a four-year school.

Students on the meandering path were worried about their parents knowing how many schools they had attended and how they were struggling. Lynn did not tell her parents that she had been disenrolled by Local State U and had started to do an online program paid for by her work: "My family has never known about this because I don't want them to think that I, you know, failed or whatever. So, I've just done this myself and it's also created a lot of anxiety for me, but it's my fault for not communicating."

Juana, who went to College Prep Charter (CPC) for high school, was accepted to four private colleges and State: "Local State U was the closest, I guess I wasn't ready to leave. A bunch of CPC students were also going to Local State U. I thought it was just the better choice, because the other ones were so far and the financial aid of private school and Local State U are different." She was accepted at schools on the East Coast, where she could major in marine biology. But she did not visit any of them and the cost of travel and living away from home deterred her from looking more into if going away to school was even possible: "Then also of course there is flying there, or how are you going to get there, and coming home, and all of that kind of stuff is an additional expense . . . but I didn't want to graduate from Local State U, I thought I'd do two years and then transfer to somewhere and get more financial aid and stuff."

But the transition to Local State U was difficult for Juana: "I was used to small classes, a small little group. Then in college it was just people everywhere, and then the classes were way bigger and I didn't really have a counselor assigned to me or anything so I was kind of on my own. I didn't really know who to reach out to, or the resources of the school." She was enrolled late in the EOP, but did not understand how it worked and missed some required workshops that she had to make up the next semester. Juana did not find her student mentor helpful and never went to ask for help or to try to change classes or her major. "I had a really bad year at Local State U with my grades and stuff. I had a really bad first semester. I only did really well in one class. Then second semester I took economics which is really hard. I ended up being disqualified so I applied to the community college."

Juana felt that her high school had really encouraged "college and stuff, and they were trying to prepare us, but I feel like the workload wasn't even close to college. And I still had in the back of my mind that I didn't want to be at State." Now in her second semester at the community college closest to her house, Juana feels like she is doing better academically: "I feel better there just because I know what to take to fill up the general education and it's not as many people as Local State U. The professors that I've had so far are not better, but I just feel more comfortable with them." Paying for school became more complicated though: "Oh that was hard because of the transition from Local State U to my community college, I had to figure out how to move my financial aid over. So, I had to pay out of pocket." Her high school counselor was able to help her move her state aid as well as her California College Promise Grant, which paid for her enrollment fees. But she did not seek help from her high school until late in the fall semester, so she was not sure if things were worked out for the start of the spring.

Emily moved around to a number of different schools and programs after graduating from a charter high school. She did not have a comprehensive record of her college units and courses completed and had no idea if she was close to getting a degree. Right out of high school she received a scholarship to attend a specialized music school, but the five-day-a-week, hour-and-a-half commute each way the first year caused her to give up the scholarship before getting a degree or certificate. She then started at a local community college but had no idea what courses to take or what she wanted to do. She became pregnant and realized she needed a quicker path to a good-paying job. She took an eight-month certificate program to be a legal assistant. The program cost about eleven thousand dollars, and she is now working forty hours a week making fifteen dollars an hour. She wanted to be able to afford housing with a yard for her child. As a result, she was commuting two hours each way to live where she could afford to rent a house. She leaves her house at five thirty in the morning, drops her child off at child care near her mother's house down the street from Saint, is at work by eight, finishes work at five, picks up her daughter, sometimes stops at her mom's for dinner, and then drives home each night, arriving between seven and eight in the evening, depending on traffic.

Students on the meandering path went through numerous transitions, and most were uncertain as to their future economic stability. They also were more likely than students on the other paths to attend an expensive for-profit school.

Work/Family Path

Students on the work/family path did not enroll in college right after high school, or did enroll for a very short amount of time and then stopped because they needed to concentrate on working full-time and/or raising children. Students on this path differed from those on the working student and meandering paths in that they did not attend multiple schools. If they tried college it was usually a local school while working, and they spent a year or less enrolled and then stopped altogether. Other students never enrolled in college, although most talked about wanting to attend at some point when they were financially settled and had the time. Close to 20 percent of all Saint alumni were on this path, and most of them had attended a public high school.

For Veronica, whom we met in a previous chapter, life circumstances meant that going to college right after high school was not an option. Because of an estrangement from her parents as well as their undocumented status, she was not able to fully complete the financial aid forms she needed to receive enough money to attend college. Further, she was struggling with homelessness and other issues that made school a lowered priority. She found a decent job that she liked and, over time, a stable place to live. She still hoped to go to school "one day," but for now is content working full-time and being with friends who support her. Saint exposed her to what was possible for her educationally. She said that she would always appreciate that Saint showed her what schools were options for her. She did not go back to Saint for help, but said she might if she decided to enroll in college later: "I did apply to four-year schools and was accepted and given some scholarships, but it was not enough, at the time I was not on speaking terms with my family and I was on my own since seventeen. So, I applied to community college and I didn't go, it was going to conflict with work. I had to survive first."

The work/family path started early for Emilio as his transition to high school from Saint was difficult. He moved high schools four times in three years, ultimately graduating from an alternative high school in his school district where college was not really talked about. He met friends there who "went into the military so I decided to join too. I used to work in fast food and I didn't want to be doing that anymore so I changed what I was doing career wise."

Emilio joined the reserves and had finished basic training the last time we talked. After coming back from boot camp, he started working two jobs in security and doing training for the reserves once a month. "My first job is in the day from 7 A.M. to 3 P.M. and my second is on weekends at night." His ultimate plan is to join the police academy. When asked what he needed to do for that, he responded, "Well what I know of is your background polygraph test then there's some counties that you need to have education. But there are some that you don't, so you can start applying just before you turn twenty-one." His boss at his security job wanted him to get more training, and so he was planning to take a mace and handcuff class, which he would have to pay for himself. Beyond friends also working in security, Emilio did not talk to anyone before making decisions about his future:

> I never really had an adult figure like that. Everyone goes to see school teachers, but I would never go talk to them on a personal level. So, it was me being independent most of the time. Once I turned fifteen I always wanted to work too. I had to wait 'til I was sixteen. . . . All my decisions and everything

I've been doing is all based on my own thoughts. My dad lives in Central America now. My mom would always allow me to transfer [high] schools. When it came time to tell her I wanted to join the military I told her and she was okay with it. . . . Basically all of my ideas I just thought of myself.

Emilio imagines his future: "I see myself pursuing my career, going to school, getting a bachelor's or master's in criminal justice, and getting a house. Helping my mom out. Starting a family."

Similarly, Martín's mom told him he needed to start paying for his own expenses when he was sixteen. She connected him with a friend who worked at a local fast-food restaurant, and he started working there full-time as soon as he could. He continued working full-time after graduating from high school.

Tatiana attended community college right after graduating from her public high school, but "wasn't really into school." She got married and had a baby, separated from her husband, and moved with her parents to a one-bedroom apartment. She was struggling to find a job that paid enough to cover her expenses as well as child care. Her hours at work changed often, and she was hoping to move from the night to the day shift and that her cousin could care for her nine-month-old. She still wanted to go back to school, but could not see how that could fit into her already full and stressful life.

Tatiana took full responsibility for her choices, saying that she was rebelling against her parents by getting married and saw now that she had made a mistake. She was thoughtful about her educational path, wondering if things would have turned out differently if her parents could have found a way to pay for her to attend the private high school she was accepted to, or supported her in attending the charter high school focused on first-generation students. But her parents wanted her to attend the traditional public high school where her brother went and "could look after me." She reflected, "I think I would have stayed more focused and actually finished college and right now I would be studying instead of being a mom and I could have waited, and be more stable now." For Tatiana, going to college was still a dream and also a point of personal failure, as she watched her friends from Saint follow the traditional and hybrid paths to college, presumably to a better, less stressful life.

Paths to College

The transition from high school to college was a difficult one for many Saint students. While academic preparation was usually not the main issue in the transition, navigating paying for college, understanding how college worked, and separating from family were challenges that Saint students faced, and most received little to no support during these transitions. The students themselves were the arbitrators of their experiences at school, while also attempting to explain the new college environment to their families. Work and the continued need for income for both themselves and their families was a constant for almost all of the students. Short-term financial considerations with limited knowledge of any other options also impacted students' eventual college decisions, and students rarely consulted advisors or financial aid directors at accepted schools.

While many high school counselors were extremely helpful in guiding students as they applied to college, once the acceptances came in there was little support for students to navigate deciding where to go and ultimately enroll, especially if there were problems with financial aid or if family situations changed in the summer after graduating from high school. Saint alumni rarely went back to high school counselors before changing their plans, and counselors did not follow-up. Students would often tell their counselor they were planning to take the expected path, of attending a traditional four-year college away from home, and then never told them when they made the decision, usually on their own, to take the hybrid traditional or working student path instead. Students felt that they were making the most rational choices for themselves and their families. Their parents thought they were working with counselors to make appropriate choices, and their counselors thought they were fine and on the best path to a college degree. And yet decisions could change dramatically from college acceptance to deposit and attendance. Students who are accepted to college but never attend are often referred to by colleges as contributing to summer "melt." This is more likely to be experienced by low-income students (Castleman and Page 2013).

Further, many students received little assistance in transitioning to college during the first year. Parents did not attend college orientations because of the language barrier, and students often did not talk much to their parents about how they were paying for and what they were doing in college. Some students on the traditional path who attended private colleges benefited from participating in first-generation college programs at their schools, while students at public four- and two-year schools were haphazardly enrolled in similar programs such as EOP (to be discussed more in the next chapter).

The first choice of college was instrumental to students staying on a path toward a bachelor's degree. As a group, students who enrolled in four-year selective schools away from home or the state school while also living at home were on the most stable paths toward a degree. Students like Isabel, on the working student path, were more mixed on their progress toward a degree and were at risk of dropping out of school if their work situation changed. Students on the meandering path were negotiating the most transitions, had the least help, and had little vision for where they were going and what to do next beyond continuing to take courses.

In the next chapter I will explore the main issues that arose for students across all of the paths post–high school, with a focus on the transition from high school to college. I will note what types of supports were helpful to students and which provided opportunities for intervention as well as which are indicators of the need for organizational and policy change. In the concluding chapter I will also discuss the ways that the structural limitations of high schools and colleges interfere with the transitional needs of first-generation college students.

5

Smoothing Pathways from Middle School to College

————————————————●

The paths that first-generation students take post–high school tell us a lot about what transitional generations need to be successful in today's educational context. Like all students striving to attend college, Saint students worked hard to take the right classes, get good grades, and be involved in different activities in high school. And many attended high schools where almost all the graduates went on to four-year colleges. But this was not enough to sustain them, as first-generation students, on the college path.

To increase degree attainment and social mobility, schools and workplaces need to examine paths to college to know where young adults get stuck and how schools and policies can be restructured. This chapter focuses on the factors that were common across the five paths that Saint students took after graduating from high school. To keep students moving toward a college degree and to transition more families to having college backgrounds, these issues must be addressed.

In the analysis of high school students in the United States presented in chapter 1, parents and students had similar expectations for college enrollment regardless of college background. However, there were areas where students differed depending on the educational backgrounds of parents. For one, FGC students were less likely to have taken the SAT or ACT by the time they were seniors in high school. This then affected their likelihood of being enrolled in a four-year college directly after high school, with almost 75 percent of continuing-generation college (CGC) students attending a four-year school compared to only 42 percent of their FGC counterparts. Further, as Langenkamp and Hoyt (2017) found, Latinas/os were much more likely to enroll in a two-year college than a four-year one, even when controlling for parents' education and socioeconomic status.

Another area of difference was the proportion of parents who thought that living at home while in college was very important. While only 18 percent of CGC parents thought living at home was important, just over 50 percent of FGC parents thought the same. These attitudes are reflected in behavior. For the national cohort of high school sophomores in 2002 who went on to college, by the spring of their second year of college, 42 percent of CGC students, 26 percent of those whose parents had some college, and only 19 percent of FGC students lived in campus-provided housing. Half of FGC students lived with their parents while going to college, compared to only 27 percent of CGC.

Parents who discourage their children from "going away" to college have been faulted for not understanding the value for their children of going to the best college they get into or the need for aspiring college students to separate from their families as young adults. Some researchers have found instances when traditional family values in Latina/o communities have resulted in young adults, especially daughters, not living on their own (Ovink 2017). While scholars often assume that differences in living at home by income or generational status may be the result of different attitudes, the paths of Saint alumni provide deeper insight into why more FGC students live at home rather than on-campus and how this affects them on the path to a college degree.

For all of the paths that students took, economic factors were paramount in students' decisions about whether or not to go away to college and involved not just the economics of paying for college, but also the need for students to work to not only support themselves but also help their families. As transitioning from high school to college also occurs at the same time that students are moving from being teenagers to young adults, this transitionary time for Saint alumni coincided with an ability to work more hours. The immediate need to pay for basic necessities interfered with their capacity to concentrate on school and threatened their ability to stay on the college path post–high school. The dual process of being the first to transition into a new educational system and progressing into adulthood when the family has few economic resources is complex and multilayered. Decisions about where to live are paramount in that cost is a driving force for FGC students attempting to obtain social mobility via higher education.

Stopping our analysis at the individual level of helping FGC students and parents make "smarter decisions" about taking the SAT, enrolling in a four-year school, moving away to attend the most selective college, and working fewer hours is an incomplete response. This approach relies on happenstance, luck, and individual behaviors, which get only a few students to a degree. But as Linda Nathan (2017) states, "Grit isn't enough." By moving beyond the individual level and not ignoring the structural realities of students' lives, we can widen the college-going path for transitional generations.

In looking at the full educational trajectories of Saint alumni, five areas emerged as important in keeping students on the path to a college degree. These five areas mattered at all stages of the educational trajectories of students, especially during the transitions between different schools. To help students at the points of transition as well as to help their whole families transition to having a college background, policy makers and educators need to address these factors.

In the rest of this chapter we examine the five areas in depth and how they played out in the lives of students from middle school to college. First, students need exposure to and then affirmation and certification of their ability to be on the college track and in the best schools in the U.S. education system. Second, students require opportunity and access to quality, inclusive schools and college preparatory curricula, especially as they are transitioning to new schools and levels of schooling. This includes a variety of types of good schools, within a reasonable geographic area. Third, students need access to people with know-how to operate and navigate in these different education systems and levels. Fourth, students need stability at home, including the economic, emotional, and physical well-being of their family members to be able to make school, and being a student, their main focus. Finally, greater attention must be paid to the reality of the many students who must work while attending high school and college.

Certification of Educational Ability in the United States

Students and parents know that Saint is a private school and that spaces at the school are limited. Parents also understand that there is a connection between the school and the church next door. The association between the school and the church reinforces the importance of education in the minds of parents, having immigrated from cultures where religion is still an important societal institution. The connection also provides a level of trust in school staff; the school has a reputation for preparing students well and, until recently, had been the only middle school in the neighborhood and thus a much-needed convenience for families. As a result, Saint receives many more applicants than it can accept. To apply, students take a placement test and are interviewed by the principal.

As a competitive process, being admitted to Saint is seen as a certification of academic ability. This is true even though Saint accepts students based not only on academic achievement but also on the assessment of staff that students have the desire to learn and that there is commitment from their parents to be involved in the school and to support their children's schooling. The experience of being accepted and then succeeding at Saint certified for students that they belonged on the college path, what Ann Mullen (2010, 108) refers to as "a deeply ingrained sense of one's place." As FGC student Suzanne said about Saint as well as her high school, "They showed me the potential that I did not know I had." This was particularly important given that almost all of the parents of Saint students were immigrants to the United States and did not necessarily understand the education system or "what it took" to go to college.

While Saint started this process of certifying students' potential to be on the path to college, this certification needed to happen at every level of the education system. The transitionary periods when students moved to new schools were particularly vulnerable times. One teacher or advisor could derail a student, as could the student encountering schools that felt very white and wealthy. Because few FGC students have people in their lives to contradict the assessments of authorities in the education system (Nichols and Islas 2016), reaffirmation at each school reminded students that they belonged on the path to college, even if they felt different from everyone else they saw on that same path.

Students who were accepted at Saint, then at a private Catholic high school known for its academic rigor and high college placement rates, and finally at a four-year college were on the ideal path to a college degree. However, struggling socially in an unfamiliar context of wealth, whiteness, and privilege in traditional private high schools as well as at four-year residential colleges made staying on this traditional college path difficult. Attending schools so demographically different from their elementary and middle schools put into question their worthiness to be at the school, even for students who were doing very well academically. Teachers at the new school, as well as a reconnection with teachers and staff from their previous school, helped to let students know that they had every right to be where they were.

The education system and the transitions between types of schools, tracks, levels of courses, and grades in general are places where students are continually judged as to their worthiness (Loveday 2016; Newkirk 2017), what Sennett and Cobb (1973) call the "hidden bar of judgement." While some Saint students continued to excel and be reaffirmed in their ability to be on the college track, there was also a flip side to certification that resulted in some students feeling extreme shame and loss of confidence in themselves when their schools told them that their grades meant that they would not be able to get into their next desired school. This happened for some students at the middle school level when Saint staff met with students and parents to let them know that their chances of getting into a private high school were small. Because students were dependent on their teachers and the school to help them with the application process, fees, and finding scholarships, students who did not have the support of Saint often did not even apply.

Gabriela was told by a teacher at Saint that her grades were not strong enough for her to get accepted at any private schools. This was impossible for Gabriela to talk about when it happened, and she hid from her friends that she was not applying to private schools: "Oh I didn't really tell them, I was like 'well, yeah I applied but I'll see once I get the letter.' You know, I didn't want to cry in front of all my friends." That experience remained difficult for Gabriela to discuss even seven years after it happened. She referred to herself as "slow" and internalized the idea that she was not smart or good enough for the private high school she wanted to attend. She then tried to get a district transfer to a public high school that had arts and activities that were more of interest to her and was denied.

For students who did apply to private high schools but were not accepted, not getting into the school of their choice provided another level of doubt and shame that was often followed by a lack of confidence and a labeling of school as "not for me." Students in this situation often stopped trying once they started at their public high schools and their grades plummeted, even though their first year of high school was "easy." They also discontinued taking courses that would keep them on the college path that Saint had started them on. These were the students most likely to be on the meandering or dead-end path post–high school graduation. For those students, it was often sophomore year when they changed their perceptions of themselves and stopped caring about school. The vulnerability for students who relied on outside organizations, teachers, and advisors means that school personnel have a lot of power to determine students' outcomes. And parents may not have the social and cultural ability to counter abuses of this power or navigate school systems in ways that are more affirming for their children (Lareau 2011).

Further, the strategy of some programs and schools to get FGC students into what are often termed "elite" schools, including private and sometimes boarding schools (Cox 2017), presumes that going to such schools is enough to create the same college track outcomes for FGC students as for CGC students. But these strategies also come with a major downside when the sorting process leaves out kids with the desire to go to college but not enough space or money to attend schools for which they qualify. Not having someone to advocate for their acceptance or funding or even know about other potential schools for which they would be a good match put those Saint alumni at a disadvantage.

On the other hand, for students like Elise, who was attending a UC, it was the consistency of Saint staff in telling her that she was "going to do great things" that got her to focus more on school while still in middle school: "At that time I literally was an attitude girl, so I had an attitude for everyone." Her grades went down in seventh grade, and there was a lot of conflict at home. But her teachers "were patient with me" and kept reminding her of what she needed to do to continue to move forward in school. Although she was waitlisted at the private high school she ultimately attended, she credits Saint with keeping her on the educational track: "My mentality changed and [the principal] would always say, 'have you done this?' So, to get supported like that along with the teachers, they pushed me to get [to college]."

Martha described her teachers and Saint staff as instrumental in her decision to attend a private high school over the public one that she knew would be so much easier: "My parents gave me my own choice [of high schools]. The principal said that he knew I struggled, because in seventh grade I struggled so much, I bombed my math test that year. And he says, 'I know you can do it. I've see you throughout these three years and how you keep working at whatever you are doing.' I was like, 'He believes in me. I know I'm going to do it.'" Martha reminded herself of the belief that Saint had in her, visited often during high school, and was on the traditional path and doing well in college, certain she would accomplish her goal of being a bilingual teacher so she could help students who struggled like she had.

Schools and school staff play an important role in certifying students' academic position and ability to be and stay on the college-going path. This certification needs to happen continually during the educational trajectories of aspiring FGC students, especially when they are transitioning between schools. Institutional support and certification by schools help students overcome the negative forces that could pull them off the college path.

Access and Opportunity

Price

The cost of private high schools deterred some Saint alumni from attending the best schools they could get into. Cost affected even more students at the college level. When I congratulated Mari on her recent graduation from a well-known private liberal arts college, she said, "thanks, expensive though." Expensive indeed. Expense was the lasting impression and experience for students in researching, planning, and finally attending college. A variety of factors were at play for high-achieving first-generation students with a desire to go to college in their decisions about where to go, but cost was paramount. In fact, for almost every student on every path, college cost was the main factor directing their decisions about which college to attend and influencing their transitional path after graduating from high school.

Students on the traditional college path needed the help of a counselor to talk with their parents about the financial aid packages they received from colleges and what it would mean for the family economically. Students did not want their parents to work even more and harder than they already did or add to their already high levels of financial stress. But understanding the financial aid packages offered by the different colleges was challenging, and students were reliant on the ability of school counselors to spend many hours with them talking about options. In the end, the students' experiences were much like those found by McCabe and Jackson (2016) with Latina/o first-generation students being very likely to figure out how to pay for college "on their own." Parents were supportive but, except for a few families, were unable to contribute toward their children's college expenses.

Most of the students who followed the traditional path to a four-year college directly out of high school, especially those who attended private colleges and lived on or near campus, had to take out loans to cover the full cost. Even though all of those students worked and had multiple scholarships, they still struggled to keep up with expenses, especially as tuition was often raised each academic year. And because their parents were not used to borrowing money in the United States, students usually did not tell their parents when they took out loans, practices that are typically suggested and assumed as necessary and normative by colleges and high school counselors. Violeta said, "The idea of loans just freak us out."

In deciding which college to attend, Arturo said, "The economic factor was huge. If [the financial aid package offered by the school] wasn't enough I said bye, bye." He ended up deciding on a UC. "When it came down to it my family would have to pay about $3,000 [a quarter]. But the first year paying $950 a month was too much. My mistake was to live on campus my second year, I was told by campus staff it would be cheaper to live on campus. And I was worried about trying to be able to have my [undocumented] parents on a lease." For his junior year he managed moving off campus with friends on his own and took a third loan to cover the thousand-dollar deposit for his share of an apartment. He said, "I do the loans myself, my parents don't need to know."

Remember Ali, who went to a private school out of state? She received grants and scholarships that covered her tuition, but she still took out over $75,000 in loans by the time she graduated college and was accruing more for graduate school. She was a best-case scenario because she found a place to live for free for two of her four years. In trying to mimic the college-going expectations of their classmates and as encouraged by their private high schools, FGC students following the traditional path stressed about finances most of their time in college. In addition, because their families were living in poverty, many of the students also needed to contribute to their families' monthly rent and other costs. Going away to college, even if the student received aid for living expenses, meant a lost contributor to the family's monthly costs. In a geographic area that both offers many different types of college options but also has extremely high rents, many incomes were necessary to rent even a one-bedroom or studio apartment.

Hoxby and Avery (2013) examine high-achieving low-income students who qualify for admittance to selective colleges but do not even apply. Early on in the article the authors dismiss the role of cost as a factor in discouraging low-income students from applying to such schools, arguing that college costs are negligible for students accepted to the most competitive colleges. Goldrick-Rab, in *Paying the Price* (2016, 239), looks at students not at selective colleges and takes a different view, stating, "Price, not intellect or effort, is the primary sorting mechanism in today's colleges and universities." In a national study of students who left postsecondary schools without a degree, 54 percent of the FGC students who left said it was because they could no longer afford it; this was also true for 45 percent of CGC students (Redford and Hoyer 2017). Cost is a factor in completion for both FGC and CGC students. For Saint alumni on the traditional path, the cost of college was a struggle for all but one student, regardless of the status and selectivity of the college they attended. Almost 80 percent of students who attended state colleges in California in 2015–2016 and borrowed money for school came from families who made less than $54,000, with the majority coming from families with incomes of $27,000 or less. Almost 60 percent of Latina/o students going to state schools had taken on debt (this percentage was 76 percent for African American students and 47 percent for whites).

Mario, who received a prestigious national scholarship that covered all expenses, was the only Saint alumni who was not working while also in college. Letty, who struggled with depression in high school, tried to take the traditional path right after high school and moved out of state. But she had no aid for living expenses her first year. She worked full-time off campus and tried to take a full course load. She failed and was dropped from many of her courses her first year. She quit her retail job when management would not allow her to come home for the winter break. When she returned for the spring semester, she pieced together a number of different jobs, but ultimately came home at the end of her first year with $5,000 loan debt and few courses she could transfer. Now she is on the working student path, enrolled at the local community college, lives with her parents and a sibling, goes to school in the mornings, and works four hours a day in the afternoons as well as more hours on weekends.

Students who took the hybrid traditional path to college altered the traditional college path by doing the math and deciding that the best strategy would be to live with their parents while working and going to college full-time. These students were on track to graduate in four to six years and would likely have little or no debt when they graduated. The strategy also allowed their parents to continue to live in the Bay Area, where wages were higher, schools and opportunities were more plentiful, and thus living at home provided more options for other members of their family to "get ahead" by being able to put more resources toward the schooling and needs of younger children.

The use of financial aid, even grants that did not need to be paid back, varied. Few students who started at a community college filled out financial aid forms, especially those who were on the meandering path. Their frequent dips in and out of schools and sporadic course taking along with the relatively low cost of community college courses made it easier for them to pay for tuition out of their own pockets. As they were working, the cost of courses did not seem like a particularly high burden. When asked if they were planning to apply for aid, they said they were "saving it" for when they went to a four-year college.

Students need to go to schools that help them get a degree in a timely manner. And they need a consistent financial aid package that gets them all the way to graduation. The year-to-year model is not efficient or effective in ensuring that students complete their degrees.

College Choice and Geography

Saint alumni needed both access to schools that matched their academic potential as well as the opportunity to attend these schools. As discussed in chapter 3, in the transition from middle to high school Saint helped as much as possible with both of these needs. Saint staff and teachers, led by the Director of Graduate Support, counseled students as to which of the private high schools would likely accept them and talked to them about back up plans in case they were not accepted. But the transition from high school to postsecondary was more complicated than the middle to high school transition. Students attended large high schools where all students were first directed to websites and given tips on how to narrow their searches among the hundreds of colleges to which they could apply. While students held on to the idealized notion of attending college directly after graduating from high school, the reality of their lives oftentimes meant that the ideal would not be realized, at least not yet. Fortunately, though, Saint students live in an area relatively rich with higher education options. There are numerous two-year community colleges, a four-year state school, and a four-year private school all within less than seven miles and easy commuting distance. But there is no UC, an affordable state option for high-achieving students.

Research has found that the transition from high school to college is influenced by the choices that students have as they are considering where to enroll, especially if they are low income. If students have public or private college options within fifty miles of where they live, they are more likely to attend and be well matched academically to the school (Dillon and Smith 2017). Having a high-quality four-year public college within commuting distance increases bachelor's degree completion rates because it diverts students from two-year schools with low retention and transfer rates; this is true even if the students start college with low skills (Frenette 2006; Goodman, Hurwitz, and Smith 2017). As Turley (2009, 141) states, "Colleges in proximity seem to increase the odds of applying to college because they make the transition to college logistically, financially, and emotionally easier." But Hillman (2016) finds that the likelihood of living close to colleges varies by race/ethnicity, with communities with a large number of Hispanic students usually having few colleges to choose from and White and Asian communities having more colleges. The flip side though is that a study of FGC students found that the farther away students went away to college, the more likely they were to complete their bachelor's degree in five or six years (Garza and Fullerton 2017).

Distance to different types of colleges is important because these factors contribute to students matching their abilities to the college they ultimately attend. First-generation and low-income students are much more likely to undermatch, or attend less selective schools than they qualify for or are accepted to (Ovink et al. 2018). This matters because students who attend colleges that are more selective are more likely to graduate, even if they are low income (Alon and Tienda 2005). But most FGC students attend schools with low graduation rates and few resources to help students transition to and then stay in college (Kelly, Howell, and Sattin-Bajaj 2016). In addition, FGC students often attend two-year schools first, but research demonstrates that if they attended a four-year school right out of high school, even if undermatched, they would be more likely to graduate (Gansemer-Topf, Downey, and Genschel 2018). Overmatching, when students are less qualified for the college they ultimately attend, is more likely to happen with students from wealthy families. These students, when overmatched, are much more likely to graduate than if they attended a school that better matched their abilities but had low graduation rates (Dillon and Smith 2017).

While the academic match between student and college is important, Kelly, Howell, and Sattin-Bajaj (2016) argue that instead of focusing on academically matching students to the appropriate institutions, we instead should be talking about overall fit. Fit includes other factors besides academics, including financial, geographic, and cultural aspects. Ultimately, quality of college is more important for issues of degree completion than match. (Goodman, Hurwitz, and Smith 2017). Thus, having good quality and affordable schools within commuting distance is important in transitioning more students to completing a college degree.

Applications and Acceptances. Most Saint students were on their own to decide where they wanted to apply to college. Suggestions were given by counselors to apply to a range of types of schools, and students were given waivers to apply to state and UC options. Sometimes the discussions between counselors and students included information about connecting interests with majors offered at the school. But once the acceptances and financial aid offers came in, students did not typically talk with their advisors before deciding. Even students who attended private high schools, where all of the graduates went on to college, did not usually work with their school counselor after they had been accepted to decide which school to attend. This was especially the case if something changed and financial aid was not working out or students were not accepted at their first-choice school. Students had picked up that their counselors thought they should attend certain schools, and they felt a sense of shame if they instead were planning to attend Local State U or a two-year school.

Students were also reticent to talk about their families' financial situation with school officials. In addition, the language barrier between parents and most of the counselors meant that many parents did not meet with anyone from school about the best college choice for their children. So while students attended a wide range of colleges, most enrolled in colleges close to home. For the full sample of interviewees who had any postsecondary experience, 63 percent went to a college where they could also live at home. Local State U provided the most affordable four-year experience. But classes and majors were impacted, and students expected to take longer then they wanted to get their degrees. For Patty, who was on the traditional path, the possible college options were widened because her older brother attended the state school out of town, where she ultimately enrolled. A good financial aid package and having family in town made her and her family feel better about her moving away from home. Her brother ultimately dropped out, but she stayed on.

Moving from Four- to Two-Year Schools. Six percent of Saint alumni who started at a four-year college transferred to a two-year school, referred to as a reverse transfer. Nationally about 16 percent of students experience a four- to two-year transfer (Liu 2016). Some Saint students who reverse transferred ended up on the meandering or dead-end path to a college degree, especially if they transferred to a community college. This group of students can teach us a lot in that many started out on the traditional path to a college degree, fully committing to this path by negotiating getting into and paying for college the first year as well as leaving home.

Students from low-income families and whose parents have lower levels of education are the most likely to experience a reverse transfer (Goldrick-Rab 2006). Goldrick-Rab finds that the impetus for such a transfer has more to do with experiences the first year of college rather than academic abilities of students before entering college. Such a transfer does not necessarily reduce the chances of struggling students ultimately graduating with a bachelor's degree (Liu 2016). This type of transfer occurred because Saint alumni could not afford the tuition of the four-year school or the cost of living away from home. Or they had started on the hybrid traditional path and then were discontinued at Local State U because of grades or finances and went to a community college to try to "get back on track." Students were often on their own as they made decisions about leaving their first college and enrolling in another school.

Know-How

In middle school Saint students learned the importance of having teachers and school staff who could help them with financial aid forms and making school-related decisions. But this support became less available the further they went in school. The most successful students sought out people to help them through their full educational trajectory or returned to Saint for any transitions. Martha appreciated that Saint helped students prepare for the transition to high school by running through "what would you do" scenarios: "What would you do if you need help from a teacher? What would you do if you have a question in class? What would you do if the class was big, small?"

The need for access to people with knowledge about the college process increases during students' educational trajectories, especially as application and financial aid forms become more complicated and deadlines as well as requirements for admission become stricter. Some middle- and high-income families have dealt with these issues by hiring private college counselors, not an option for most FGC students due to the cost. Lareau (2015) notes that students need a "cultural guide" to get what they need out of their high schools as well as to navigate the college choice, application, and enrollment processes. But those guides could not just be anyone. Saint students were helped most by cultural guides who had also been members of a transitional generation. Saint purposefully employed staff who had taken a similar journey as a first-generation student. And then in high school students relied very heavily on teachers and counselors, especially to navigate the mysterious process of applying to college. In those school contexts where most of the staff was white and had gone to college, students leaned heavily on any staff who could relate to their experience, and in the absence of such persons appreciated counselors who made an effort to understand their experience. Or students went back to Saint for help. Xochi talked about the importance of an older Saint alumnus who became her mentor through high school and college.

Jeanne went back to Saint after she was not accepted to any of the state schools to which she applied. The principal at Saint helped her pick a community college with the highest transfer rate. Then during her first year at the college, her English professor helped her to enroll in three linked courses that included advising with the professor of one of the courses: "And I would talk to that professor and her colleague that she referred me to mostly for any academic questions and to plan my track and see how to transfer, and that was really helpful." Getting connected in the first year helped with the transition to college and kept Jeanne on track, and she did transfer to a four-year school in three years. Such experiences were usually because of luck in whom students met their first year in college.

Although FGC students would benefit the most from programs and services offered by their schools, they are more likely to attend schools that are financially stretched and may not provide such supports. Further, FGC students are less likely to utilize such services compared to CGC students

(Atherton 2014). In college, FGC students are also less likely to interact with faculty or to work with faculty on research (Kim and Sax 2009), one of the "high impact" practices in college that increases student outcomes and satisfaction with college. Further, Latina/o students have limited academic contact with peers. For CGC students, the size of the class did not matter in predicting their interactions with faculty or having conversations with peers in class. Individuals as well as schools and programs can help students in planning for and then transitioning from high school to college. However, increasing class size is a strategy of state schools to manage the demand and deal with shrinking state budgets, strategies that could alienate FGC students even further (Beattie and Thiele 2015).

The Power of Individuals

The notebook at Saint that visitors sign in and out of is full of the names of volunteers who come and go each day. They include high school and college students doing service hours, adults from the local community who know about the school through their friends on the school's board, and members from Catholic churches and schools who know about Saint and usually attend their fund-raisers. One such volunteer was instrumental in helping Ali. Because she was good at math and Saint did not have multiple levels of math, the school found a personal tutor to work with her during her scheduled math class. The tutor was a mom, Ms. C, who believed in the values of Saint and volunteered with the school. She had two daughters who attended one of the private high schools. Said Ali,

> Ms. C. was my math tutor, she was teaching me geometry when I was in eighth grade. We'd have these one-on-ones and she would talk about the high school where her daughters went. She said that if I went there she'd be my donor and my sponsor, and she was, for four years. So I had that connection and she just told me about what a wonderful opportunity it was and when I shadowed at the high school I really liked the style of teaching and how they encouraged thinking and it was very similar to Saint in terms of the Catholic feel, so I felt welcomed.

The importance of "linked lives" in life course theory is evident in the stories of many Saint alumni who stayed on the college path. And often those initial links continued to snowball into connections with other individuals, many of whom served as "cultural guides" through students' transitions to different schools. After she graduated from high school, a story about Ali in her high school newsletter caught the attention of another parent who had just moved to the town where Ali was going to college. The parent's family became Ali's "second family," with whom she lived for free for two years. That family introduced her to the family for whom she became a nanny and lived with during graduate school. The connections to families with financial resources and knowledge of college and who also encouraged her to have as full a college experience as possible helped to keep Ali on the traditional college path.

To activate this social capital and form relationships across race, social class, and educational backgrounds, students needed to learn how to build relationships on their own, without relying solely on their parents to help them. In his book *Privilege*, Shamus Khan (2011) shows how a boarding school deliberately cultivated these relationships and socialized elites into the cultural norm of feeling comfortable speaking with adults and expecting help from authority figures. Many alumni noted that that was something they learned at Saint, and even though it was not a boarding school, the seven o'clock start time and shared meals were important times for building relationships with teachers and staff. Said Violeta,

> And it was a learning experience to sort of feel comfortable asking for help, but I think that also a part of it that made it so easy to ask for help was that the teachers and volunteers and basically the whole faculty [at Saint] just made it really easy to feel like you could go talk to them for anything. And we spent so much time with them outside of the classroom where it almost felt like they were another friend or like another family member. It was easy to go talk to them. We would have, every day when we would have breakfast, a faculty member would be there. There was at least one faculty would sit at our table and we talked to them. So, we got to form, and it was kind of forced, those relationships outside of the classroom too. So, when it came to asking for help later, it felt easier. And then I mean for me like now, even going to [high school] where I could have that opportunity to create those same sort of relationships and I did, it just made it so much easier to create those—I mean I don't know if you'd call them friendships, but just to create those relationships where it's easy to be like hey, I need help in this, which then helped me now that I'm in college because they are very heavy on office hours and then going into your professor's office and having conversations with them and asking

them for help. And I think if I had not gotten that opportunity to sort of feel comfortable talking to a teacher early on, then it would definitely be harder to do it now that I'm older. But because I kind of got to feel comfortable doing that since I was smaller, it just makes it easier to do it now.

This skill became extremely important when Violeta's college financial aid package was lessened her sophomore year and she had to work up the nerve to meet with someone in the college's financial aid office. She kept putting off going until a faculty member she was working with encouraged her to go: "So I was like, yeah, you're right, I can do this." The financial aid officer helped her better understand her package, and she was actually able to take out a lower loan because of that meeting.

Violeta also maintained her relationship with staff at Saint. When she was a high school student the graduate support director and president of Saint took her to visit Stanford because she had never been there. And the former principal had friends who were college counselors who helped her with her financial aid forms along with her high school advisor. These linked lives, across the different schools students attended, helped smooth paths to college. Students valued the opportunity to keep their relationships with influential teachers and staff at Saint even through their high school years, coming back to ask for help in math and for other types of support.

For Mateo, that cultural guide was his high school counselor, whom he first met through a summer program for potential FGC students when transitioning from middle to high school. Mr. J. stuck with Mateo his whole time in high school, helping him figure out his strengths and then prepare for his transition to college:

> At first, I really wanted to do math, and [Mr. J.] realized right away that the only reason that I chose math was because that's the only thing I knew, really the only thing I thought I was good at. So then he was what do you like to do, what are your hobbies, what's something you actually want to explore? That's when I fell in love, I enjoy fooling around with computers, figuring out what they actually do. That's when he's like have you considered the idea of computer science? And I told him, no, I had not. I didn't even know what that was back then.

Mateo enrolled in his first high school computer science class and was hooked. Then Mr. J. helped him figure out the best colleges for the field. Mateo applied to fourteen schools:

I didn't go visit schools until I got accepted. I did get into nine schools, but I couldn't make the effort to visit all nine. Especially when I was a first-generation student, I couldn't really afford the plane travel and everything to go to all these different schools. So what my counselor did, he told me, you know what, if they're willing to accept you then they obviously see something in you, so let's see if they'll fly you out over there. So he emailed every school that I got into and told them, "Well here's the situation. He would love to come and visit your school but he can't afford the plane travel. Would you mind flying him out and showing him around for the weekend?"

One school said yes. Another school was a three-hour drive from Mateo's home. Mr. J. drove him to visit: "So he took a day out of his weekend to actually drive me all the way down to show me around the school." Mateo ultimately decided that was the school he wanted to attend.

Luckily for Mateo, Mr. J. stayed at the high school during his whole time as a student there and has also been available for him to check back in with since graduating. But such connections are rare and staff in schools and programs are not as reliable as family. This makes FGC students, reliant on such ties for guidance over their full educational trajectory, at a disadvantage compared to CGC students who can usually activate the social capital in their informal/familial networks when they need it. FGC students relied on teachers and school staff who were willing to go over and above their job descriptions to help them, a very individual solution to a structural need for FGC students.

Organizations and Programs Providing Know-How

Students are able to activate the know-how of individuals when the structure of the schools they attend allows for such connections to take place. High school advisors who met students while in middle school or over the summer before high school and stayed with them throughout their time were ideal situations, such as the case of Mateo. The graduate support director at Saint as well as other Saint staff were also touchstones for students as they transitioned to high school as well as when they prepared for their next transitions post–high school graduation. Being able to consult with staff at Saint was particularly important when students did not feel a connection to or get the help they needed from their high school counselors.

Oftentimes the job descriptions for teachers and advisors do not include substantial time to help graduates. While some students may ask for recommendations or stop by their previous school to say hello, usually school staff are too busy with the next cohort of current students to spend much time reaching out to past students. The position of graduate support director at Saint was dedicated to just this purpose. And it was a huge job as every year more and more students wanted help. This person also needed to stay up to date with anything that former students might need. Requests might include accessing GI Bill benefits, applying for a DREAM scholarship in California, and so forth. The director would also hold summer workshops for students and parents about the college application process and would manage the after-school space where high school students could continue to come to do their homework after they graduated.

Similarly, high schools need to develop both "organizational norms and structures that guide students effectively through the college application process" (Roderick, Coca, and Nagaoka 2011, 178). People who serve as "organizational brokers" in schools can help students transition to their new school and also provide opportunities for people to connect across networks. These "weak ties" (Granovetter 1973) can be very valuable in providing connections that could lead to internships, jobs, or even affordable places to live and ultimately increase the social capital of those who utilize these weak ties. Even though not the ultimate goal of a school, social ties for students may become happy by-products of programs and very useful for students who do not have social capital.

Programs for underrepresented students during high school and/or college can also help to fill in existing resources and information for students whose parents are not able to help them with educational issues and transitions (Davenport 2016; Swail 2000) and are necessary in today's college environment to increase equity in college enrollment and completion across background. Precollege programs usually include supports for students in seeing college as an option, applying to college, and then helping with their college choice. These programs have shown varying levels of success, partially because follow-up with graduates has been difficult (Perna 2002; Valentine et al. 2011). Parental involvement is often one key component of programs that focus on students while they are in middle and high schools, and the incorporation of parents is one area that programs attempt but often have a difficult time maintaining (Ceja 2006). Low-income youth have much better academic outcomes when their parents are involved at their school (Benner,

Boyle, and Sadler 2016). This is also true for college access programs for Latina/o students (Auerbach 2004; Wartman and Savage 2008).

Swail (2000) notes that many programs for aspiring first-generation students are often separate from schools themselves and need to do more to connect to actual schools. This kind of smoothing is necessary as potential FGC students may be involved in different types of programs both within and independent of their schools, and it becomes incumbent on students to try to figure out how to get their needs met and access resources across programs, something that parents likely do for CGC students. As Hamilton (2016, 197) emphasizes, programs to help FGC students get into college must continue once students enroll in college: "If the goal is to narrow the gap in educational opportunity, universities need to provide disadvantaged youth with the same tailored guidance and financial support that affluent, highly educated parents provide for their offspring."

Patty, on the traditional path but who almost dropped out of her state school because she felt like she did not belong, credits the Equal Opportunity Program (EOP) for keeping her in college: "If it wasn't for EOP I don't think I would still be here. Because they talked about a lot of stuff, they talk about financial aid, they talk about school, they talk a lot about culture shock, which I think was really interesting and really helpful at this school, and also about getting used to your environment." She met her best friends at college via EOP, and her EOP advisor was very approachable: "He was amazing and such a good help. I went in one time and I was having an issue with my roommates and I was kinda stuck in that, everyone had more money than me, was better than me, and I had a couple of people be rude with me and I felt it was because I was different. And I went to talk to him and I could always just be so honest with him and he really helped." For Yesenia, the EOP provided her with a mentor, a more advanced student in her major who helped her with course choices and navigating the requirements of the major.

Programs are also being developed to help FGC students with transitions from college to career. For example, the Braven program provides students with a career-planning class and most importantly connects students with mentors in their chosen career area, what they call "building a rich uncle network" in an attempt to mimic the social capital inherent in many CGC students' families.

Juana, who was on the meandering path after being disenrolled at Local State U, said, "I feel like colleges should have maybe a club or group made for them besides EOP. Then for the transition also, like a college program, to learn about the resources on campus, because I had no idea." Juana thought that the summer programs she did before starting Saint and before she started at College Prep Charter High School were very helpful and would have helped during her first semester as a college student at Local State U.

Availability of Know-How When Most Needed

Cultural guides were vital when students most needed them, not necessarily when programs or advisors suspected they were most needed. Often the guides were most essential during the transitions between schools, especially when students went from a school where staff could communicate with their parents in Spanish to schools where there were few or no staff available. Students often adjusted to these situations by taking care of school things on their own and assuring their parents that everything was fine.

As we saw in the experience of Ali, who had good social capital with college knowledge, she still needed to be able to access know-how when she was struggling with college-related decisions, such as her major. Being able to access people with specific knowledge at crucial points in their college adjustment was extremely important and was not usually available to students. If students were struggling in a class, with course registration, or with negotiating their job hours and class times, they needed a trusted mentor to reduce the risk of dropping out. Know-how was especially needed by students as they made decisions about their major and career interests. Choice of major and guided course taking has been found to be important in retaining students and getting them to graduation (Bailey et al. 2016). The real issue is the need to focus on improving access to people with know-how at the colleges where most FGC students attend. These are often big, public colleges with low graduation rates. Some states have been working to improve the rates of retention, credit completion, and graduation at public institutions (such as Tennessee and Indiana [College Equity Report 2018]). Results are just beginning to come in and have been mixed depending on the type of intervention.

Many students on the meandering path faced problems because they had trouble passing one course. More than one student reported taking the same class three times because they thought they had to for their major or general education requirements. Students at the community colleges were often paying for the classes themselves, and they never talked to an advisor to see if there were other options. Ultimately, they dropped out or were forced to stop because of a hold put on their account for financial or advising issues. Some students who were having trouble passing courses at Local State U were ultimately disenrolled. Students were uncertain about what they would need to do to be able to reenroll and felt discouraged about their ability to do well in college overall. All of the students in this situation talked about eventually returning to school, but they had no specific plans to do so.

For the students who had done well in high school, even getting a C felt like failure. Because they were used to getting good grades, they wanted to "do over" any course in which they struggled. But that was unrealistic given difficulties in finding space in those courses as well as paying to take the course again. Students tried to remedy such situations by going to a different college, ultimately finding themselves in the same predicament as before. For each student, the path to each of these colleges became a dead-end. This was particularly painful for students who had done well academically in middle and high school. Marta said this about her first year at Local State U: "I did really bad. And it was kind of hard for me because at high school I had like a 4.3, or a 4.0, so it's been really hard to not do well in college. It's been kind of rough taking that all in."

Students on the meandering and dead-end path were accruing debt or had paid out of pocket for courses that ultimately were not counting toward a degree. They were lost in a cycle of shame and despair for not planning better, getting one bad grade, or not being able to figure out what courses to take. Students in two-year colleges who had graduated from a private high school also appeared to be worse off than those who graduated from a public or charter school. The private schools rarely or never talked about community college as an option and what degrees and certificates were possible. For Samuel, a girlfriend told him what an associate's degree was. In a study of FGC and CGC students at community colleges in California it was found that FGC students, compared to CGC students, were less satisfied with their access to and the usefulness of services offered by the school, even though both groups used services at similar rates (Shumaker and Wood 2016). This suggests that community colleges may need to do more to understand what FGC students need from the services offered and evaluate where such services may be falling short.

The need for connections with those with know-how is not ancillary; FGC students who meet with an academic advisor are much more likely to be retained in college (Swecker, Fifolt, and Searby 2013). In fact, at the public research university where that study took place, *each* meeting with an advisor increased the likelihood of FGC students staying in college by 13 percent.

Family Stability and the Transition to Adulthood

The stability of students' families was a crucial factor in their decisions about postsecondary attendance. Coming from a family with a stable income and housing arrangement as well as the ability to care for other family members allowed students to make educational choices that were best for them. But many students came from families that did not have such stability. The situation is mainly the result of wages being tied so tightly to education level. As we saw in chapter 1, in California 48 percent of adults with less than a high school degree live in poverty, including 26 percent of Latinas/os who are poor. Latinas/os have the highest poverty rate of any race/ethnicity that is measured using the California Poverty Measure (Wimer et al. 2018). Most of the alumni from Saint are in families where their parents have less than a high school degree and live below or near the poverty line.

When Family Needs You

Economists who have been puzzled by the low application rate to selective colleges of high-achieving students from low-income families have assumed that the main issue is lack of knowledge about the generous aid available at many private schools. Attempts to increase students' informational capital have been marginally successful in gaining more applicants from low-income families. Unless understanding is widened to consider the whole family, researchers will continue to be confused about why students are not making the seemingly rational, independent choice to attend the most highly ranked college, no matter where it is located. Even if selective schools provide full-ride scholarships and grants, without addressing the potential economic insecurity of the students' whole families, the highest achieving but most economically vulnerable students will be unlikely to attend such schools, regardless of how generous the financial aid package is. This was demonstrated most explicitly in the college enrollment patterns of Saint alumni on the hybrid path who chose the school that was most economical

(Local State U) and lived at home where, because of their transition to adulthood, they could also work and contribute more to rent and other family expenses. Removing these students from the household would have had damaging economic effects on the whole family, and, as we saw for those students who took the traditional path, caused them to be in debt.

The role of family need was particularly noticeable in the experiences of alumni from single-parent families. Although children in single-parent families usually have lower educational and occupational outcomes compared to children raised in two-parent families (Amato 2005), for Saint students being part of a single-parent family was not necessarily the most important factor in determining outcomes. Rather, when there were younger siblings also in the family and the eldest child was a Saint alumnus, the alumnus usually had more caretaking responsibilities for siblings when there was only one parent. However, for those who were only children or had older siblings, being raised in a single-parent household did not interfere with their educational goals as long as the parent had a stable job over time. In fact, alumni would note the extreme sacrifices of their single parent as a major motivating force in graduating from college. Alex said his mom was his main motivation and did everything she could to make sure that he did not work too much so he could make school his number one priority. Her stable job at an event center for many years combined with a second part-time job allowed Alex to focus on school and work only during vacations and summers. On the hybrid path, he was on track to graduate from Local State U in five years with no debt.

Parents' stable health was also important. For Marta, a sudden health crisis with her father during high school caused added stress and continued to threatened her ability to stay on the hybrid path. Concern about the health of family members interfered with the educational trajectories of many Saint alum. Students on the work/family path had the heaviest caretaking responsibilities for disabled parents or their own children. Students balancing work and family responsibilities were not able to cut back on either to focus more on their postsecondary goals. Needing to work long hours and take care of family members puts such students at an extreme disadvantage for finishing college compared to students without such responsibilities (Ziskin et al. 2010). Child care is a particular need for the many students of nontraditional age who are attempting to go to school for postsecondary training (Berman 2018). Nationally, nearly five million college students in the United States are raising children while they go to college. In the six most western states, including California, 22 percent, or more than 700,000 undergraduate students, are also parents (Noll, Reichlin, and Gault 2017).

Further, as first- and second-generation immigrants, Saint students were also the cultural bridge to the United States for their families and a form of social capital for their parents in that they needed to communicate important messages to their parents about their own educations, and their parents also relied on them to accompany them to medical and other appointments as well as to fill out forms and interact with school systems for their other children. As a result, children were the conduits to many formal relationships for parents. These "language brokering responsibilities may clash with the self-focused nature of emerging adulthood" (Weisskirch 2017, 17) and can result in academic stress for Latina college students (Sy 2006).

For emerging adults, being a language broker for parents can bring parents and adult children closer together, but can also interfere with the young adults' need to participate in more self-focused activities and could limit youths' sense of life possibilities (Dorner 2017; Weisskirch 2017). The expectation to continue to help parents in this way goes against the assumption of colleges that students can focus primarily on their own development, especially by moving away for school. While children's language brokering activities typically decrease as they age, second-generation adults continue to play an important role in helping their parents (Dorner 2017; Vallejo 2012; Yoo and Kim 2014). Language brokering is a distinct skill (Weisskirch 2017) that children develop over time and helps them to form empathy for others and also build relationships with adults in formal roles.

More recent theorizing about how social capital is developed and maintained is beginning to show not only that parents are a potential beneficial source of social capital for children, but also that children can be a potent source of social capital by introducing their parents to the parents of their friends and classmates (Offer and Schneider 2007). This is an understudied area of research, with schools needing to "be more sensitive to the complexity of familial processes" (Offer and Schneider 2007, 1137).

At the same time, the role of parents, regardless of income, has long been recognized as an important force in the educational trajectories of children, including the transition to postsecondary options (Gofen 2009; Kim and Díaz 2013; Kim and Schneider 2005; Swail and Perna 2002). However, high expectations and support are not enough when parents are faced with the everyday reality of economic survival.

As we saw in chapter 3, a challenge has been to continue to keep parents involved in students' educational lives as they are increasingly being influenced by teachers and other school officials. This is particularly difficult when students' parents do not speak the same language as those teachers and administrators (Lee et al. 2012; Orellana 2003, 2009), which was the case for the majority of Saint students. Because Saint consciously employed staff who spoke Spanish and English, parents could be very involved in the academic lives of their children while they were in middle school. However, once students transitioned to high school, there were fewer individuals that parents could communicate with. This was particularly true when Saint students attended private high schools where there was no designated liaison between students, parents, and the school. Unless students happened to attend a school where a Spanish-speaking teacher or counselor was on staff, students were on their own to communicate to their parents about their educational experiences.

Legal Status of Students and Parents

Not having authorization to live in the United States posed problems in the transition to different schools for both students and their families as well as students' ability to leave their families to go away to college. Until they could figure out whom to trust as well as the application requirements at the different colleges, students and parents needed to be cautious about revealing their status. Regina noted, "I think in middle school [your status] never really comes up. But one time the [grad support director at Saint] had a meeting for undocumented students, and I saw a big group of people. I think in middle school nobody talks about it. I feel like it's really not an issue until you get into high school, because I've never felt any different because of it." But her status was important once she was in high school, applying to college and trying to figure out what types of financial aid she may be eligible for: "I feel like I taught my [high school] counselor more than she taught me. I know that I was not the first one who was undocumented, and then she said that nobody had ever told her their status. She's grateful that I actually opened up to her. I was like, 'I don't really have a problem telling people. It is what it is.'"

All of the students interviewed who were undocumented had Deferred Action for Childhood Arrivals (DACA) status at the time of the interview. The passage of DACA in 2012 changed the lives of emerging adults dramatically. Although it did not provide a path to citizenship, it did allow students to work legally, travel more freely, and participate in activities at college. For students who were undocumented, getting DACA status was the key to opening up their working lives. When asked about the cost of getting and renewing DACA ($500), Regina said, "But for me it is worth it, because I can work. I got my ID and then my driver's permit right away. I got my driver's license. I got a job." DACA also helped students feel safe enough to reveal their status, which allowed those with know-how, including teachers and counselors at school, to help them more and let them know about scholarships and potential internships. Although at the time of this writing the Trump administration is trying to revoke DACA, for the most part students were not worried about their own status. They were more worried about their parents and what would happen if they were deported. This affected a large number of Saint students in that most were second-generation immigrants, born in the United States but whose parents were born in Mexico or Central America, and many did not have protected status to live in the United States.

Students lived with the possibility of their parent or parents being deported at any time. Said Isabel, "My mom she's undocumented and she's the only one who's in charge of me and my siblings because my dad is out of the picture. And she works all over the Bay Area and you know not every city is safe, so she's definitely a lot more careful now when she's driving anywhere. And when she accepts different jobs, she'll try and be aware, like we heard on the news that ICE agents would call independent contractors to go to certain locations and catch them there. So she's been definitely a lot warier about working." Although the potential of deportation has always been a concern for families, students were more scared now: "Before we weren't super cautious about it, like if there was a tail light broken on the car, we'd be like, 'Oh, we'll fix that eventually.' Now we're like, 'we got to get that fixed immediately.'"

Families handled the reality of possible deportation in different ways. Some parents were very direct with their older children, telling them the plan if they were deported, where they would live, and who would take care of them. For the few who owned their own homes, the oldest children would have the responsibility of raising their younger siblings. In other families, the parents acknowledged the possibility but did not really talk about it. Said Juana, "I feel that I'm the most worried of everyone. I feel nervous every time my dad leaves for work on his bike." Students texted their parents if they heard about ICE raids in certain areas. Rachel was most worried about her community and her younger siblings:

It's just horrible seeing so many families that are terrified, they're scared—
they're scared that immigration is going to come and take them away and
their kids who are born here are going to stay here and going to foster care
and like you know, things like that. It's just scary and I remember when
[Trump] got elected, my siblings started to cry. They're like I don't want
Mamí and Papí leaving. I don't want them taking them away. And it didn't
make me cry because it's like they're not going to take them away. It is a huge
possibility though that it can happen but it's just sad seeing that my
siblings—even my siblings are watching this. You know watching it from the
media from like Snapchat, Instagram all this media—this social media that
it's like just sad that they're like recognizing how like the politics effects like
everyone . . . they're scared and my parents always calm them down like
nothing's going to happen to us and if anything does happen to us you know,
we have other family members here that we can take you to or since I'm
already eighteen, you know, I can take care of them, but it's still super hard.

The threat of deportation was also something that influenced the whole
neighborhood where Saint students lived.

Neighborhood

As students became older and traveled outside their community to attend
high schools in more wealthy areas, they started to become more aware of
the issues in their neighborhood. Some became more concerned about their
siblings and parents and wished they could do something to move their
whole family to a safer area. Yesenia said, "The neighborhood has not
changed, it's just stuff that I've realized because I'm growing up. The violence, that's very prevalent in the area. Gang violence. I think it's always been
there, it's just something that my parents would not tell me because I was
young. It's stuff that I'm starting to see on my own now."

Rachel remarked, "I wanted to move out of this neighborhood so bad. I
love, I love everyone here but there it's just sometimes it's like 'why are we here?'
We need to leave. When we go to [a wealthy neighborhood a few miles away] and
all of a sudden, it's a rich neighborhood and it annoys me so much and it bothers
me that my mom, we can't survive in a good neighborhood." Students dreamed
about becoming successful in their future jobs and being able to "help my parents" by buying them a house in a "good neighborhood."

Work

Paid work was an essential part of the lives of all but one of the students interviewed for this project. As mentioned before, Mario had a generous scholarship and worked only on school breaks. His family was also financially stable enough so he did not need to send money home. All of the other students worked, some at multiple jobs. Nationally 75 percent of undergraduate students who are claimed as dependents typically work while attending college. They work an average of twenty-four hours a week (Perna, Cooper, and Li 2010). However, the type of work differs by the social class background of the parents, with students from upper-class families more likely to work in career-related internships and students from low-income families working in low-paid service jobs that are not related to their college majors (Carnevale and Smith 2018).

A substantial proportion of students work full-time; 32 percent of students enrolled at public two-year colleges work full-time while enrolled in classes, while 18 percent of students at four-year colleges do so (Velez, Bentz, and Arbeit 2018). But earnings from work can diminish the amount of aid that students receive, essentially counting against them in the financial aid calculus (Perna 2002).

For students balancing work and school, the types of jobs they could get, wages, and flexibility of hours as their school schedules changed each quarter or semester were all important factors for students both in high school and in college. While excelling academically and being involved in sports at high school, Ali held a number of jobs:

> Well, I originally started working because my parents needed help, but then by my senior year it was more because I wanted to cover the little expenses that I knew my parents couldn't get me like a cell phone and stuff. I've had a lot of different jobs, I used to work special events, and I worked at a water park, and my mom is a house cleaner so I used to clean houses with her too and my dad did landscaping so I would help him sometimes on special projects, and babysitting. I was also a tutor for a few students who were in middle school and worked with a child with special needs.

Ali continued this strategy of working multiple jobs when she went away for college, sending money home when she could and covering all of her own living expenses as well.

Wages connected with the kinds of jobs that students can get are important. Many Saint alumni worked at fast-food restaurants while in high school, and those who stayed in the area on the working student path kept working in fast food, even though their hours were not always compatible with school. Students on the traditional path were more likely to work on campus, often starting in the cafeteria. Said one alumnus, "No one wants to leave the library jobs which are the best for getting your work done, so I had to take what I could get." But for students who had the most financial stressors, working on campus was limiting as they could work only a certain number of hours and the pay was stagnant. Jeanne started working at the school cafeteria because she did not have a car and needed a job on campus. A side benefit of the job was that she made friends with the other students she was working with: "So I work in culinary services and the first friend I made was actually there. And so I made friends with her friend group."

Jeanne could work a maximum of twenty hours a week on campus, which she did most semesters: "But it's not enough financially for rent and everything, but it is enough [hours] with the academic load that I have to work with." Said Ali about why she quit the retail and campus jobs she had in college and started babysitting instead, "That's how I ended up putting myself through college and obviously, the minimum wage was like $8.75 at the time and I had a few part-time jobs, but it wasn't enough to cover everything and that's how I got into babysitting. So, I've been with the family that I am with now for three and a half years." Living and working on campus resulted in a very stressful situation for Arturo. Once he could move to a cheaper living arrangement off campus, he was able to keep his campus job while enrolled in classes and then increase his earnings with weekend and summer work at Home Depot.

Students on the hybrid and working student paths were the most likely to work off campus and at jobs they had since high school. Often students worked at the same places that other Saint alumni did, having referred each other.

A major difference between working while in high school versus college is that in high school class usually ends at the same time each day. But in college student schedules change at least two times a year. In California, where many schools are on the quarter system, schedules change more often. As a result, students are very dependent on their jobs to give them flexibility to concentrate on school when they need to. When Gabriela stopped attending her community college to go to a trade school, she appreciated the fixed hours of the program. She chose the evening session and worked at Starbucks in the mornings: "I'd start at four in the morning and then work until ten or eleven, then start studying and sometimes take a nap, and then go to school from five to ten P.M., and then just do it all over again."

Students going to school and living at home had an advantage over those who moved away to go to school in that they could usually keep their retail jobs and continue to work during school breaks, sometimes the best time to make money. To graduate more FGC students, more needs to be done to help them balance working while going to school (Carnevale and Smith 2018; Perna, Cooper, and Li 2010).

Conclusion

As shown in this chapter, students are usually on their own to figure out how to stay on the path to college, even when stressors are pulling them off track. To be able to graduate more students requires that a number of problems in the U.S. education system be addressed. If states and the United States want to move more FGC students to achieving a degree, addressing these issues needs to become a priority.

Along their educational trajectory, students need exposure to and then affirmation and certification of their belonging on the college track, especially when experiencing culture shock. This certification must continually be reaffirmed, specifically when students change schools. Next, students require opportunities and access to quality schools and the paths necessary to get into and stay in these schools, especially as they are transitioning to new schools and levels of schooling. This includes being able to reasonably pay for and have a choice of schools that match their abilities and interests. Third, students need people and organizations as well as programs that understand them and whom they trust, that can consistently provide knowhow as students navigate new schools. Fourth, more support is needed for families living in poverty so that students can go to school and not worry as much about the economic well-being of their families. Finally, greater attention must be paid to the reality of students who must work while attending college and to help students find good jobs that will also allow them to move forward in college rather than interfering with their educational progress.

6

The Journey Before Us

First-Generation College
Students and College
Completion

It is September and a new cohort of sixth graders and their families are in the school cafeteria, being welcomed to Saint Middle. OUR FUTURE is painted in large letters on the wall above them, surrounded by college banners from Fordham, University of Oregon, University of San Francisco, and many others. Parents are proud to have a coveted spot at the middle school and believe that education will pave the way to better futures for their children. They trust Saint to help their children realize this dream.

The teachers and staff at Saint know that they can move students academically beyond their grade level, and that by the time students graduate the majority will be prepared to do well at the most rigorous high schools in the area. The students are more unsure; they know they have long days and summers of schoolwork ahead, yet this apprehension will last only a few weeks as they adjust to the new schedule and make connections with their teachers and classmates.

But as we have seen in the previous chapters, to transition aspiring first-generation students onto the college path in the twenty-first century takes more than parents, students, and perhaps even teachers understand. As the students profiled in this book demonstrate, for even the most determined and academically gifted students, the path from poverty to being the first in their family to graduate high school in the United States and then on to college is difficult. Strong individual attributes are not enough to ensure that students can, on their own, stay on the path to a college degree.

As a country we have allowed our schools, educational systems, and neighborhoods to be highly segregated by race, social class, and privilege (Cottom 2017; Lee 2005; Lewis and Diamond 2015; Nunn 2014). As a result, students have unequal access to the resources necessary to get a college degree (Nathan 2017). This is occurring both within and between schools as we saw from the experiences of Saint alumni. Even in relatively "good" public schools, alumni were put on less demanding academic paths, though they were capable of much more (Lewis-McCoy 2014; Ochoa 2013). And at the academically rigorous private schools, students missed out because of their parents' inability to understand and ask for resources such as AP courses and help with college choice decisions as well as when financial aid or other issues changed students' college plans (Calarco 2018; McDonough 1997). Further, an unequal distribution of public resources has allowed for the growth and development of for-profit schools, which are not universally positive for the mainly low-income students who go to such colleges (Cottom 2017).

To have more students complete college, the United States needs to embrace the collective journey it will take to restructure our schools and pathways to college. The alumni from Saint realized that their journey to college was much bigger than they were. But the structure of complex societies does not honor this fuller journey. Students are passed from school to school, participate in a variety of programs, and meet many adults along the way which allows them to easily slip off track without being noticed. We have designed the path to college to move students on rather than take the journey with them, and this is reflected in how teachers, counselors, and other knowledgeable adults' jobs are structured.

Many psychologists are focusing on the role of grit, defined as having the stamina to persevere and work hard, even when faced with barriers (Duckworth 2016). The continuing-generation college students of today are beneficiaries of a relative who was the transitional generation for their family and was gritty in the past. That, combined with a structure that offered affordable college, a more generous social safety net, and stable jobs, enabled their hard work to translate into social mobility.

Grit and hard work continue to be necessary. However, in today's structure of expensive postsecondary options, jobs that do not pay a wage that students can live on, and segregation of school quality by race and social class, grit does not meet a compatible opportunity structure for success. Grit helps when working full-time while attending a residential four-year school but is not enough when students also need to pick up their siblings from school each day, help parents pay the rent, and be available to translate at parents' medical appointments. And the amount of grit they have does not matter when students are transitioning to different schools and do not even know what questions to ask, such as about taking college-prep courses or how many units are necessary to graduate on time. Grit only goes so far when a child is sick, a paper is due, and students will be fired if they do not show up for work. If we focus only on grit we will never solve the college completion crisis, especially for students who are born into low-income families (Nathan 2017).

If nothing changes in the context of the economic and educational inequalities that exist in the United States today, college completion will be linked to grit for some and with highly involved parents with social and cultural capital who pull their children through school for others. The structure and culture of schools and acceptable paths to college must change.

To increase the proportion of college graduates in the United States, we cannot rely on past strategies. We can learn from the successes of programs and schools such as Saint and then look at the barriers that members of transitional generations face to design better systems and wider paths for students. The rest of this chapter summarizes the main findings in *The Journey Before Us* by each system level in need of change to more concretely realize the collective journey before us.

Schools as Part of the Journey

At Saint Middle School, students became aware of their academic potential. The goal was set for them to attend the best high school that in turn would ensure a smooth path to a bachelor's degree. Students and parents alike understood these goals and were committed to the path set out for them. Saint prepared them to do well academically in high school and helped them to apply to the best high schools to continue to grow their potential. What Saint Middle did was provide a place where students believed in that potential and gave them the academic rigor they needed to succeed in high school and college. Further, Saint supported and celebrated their identities as first-generation students and children of immigrants, valued and included their parents by partnering with them in educating their children, and made sure parents could speak directly with school administrators and most of the teachers.

Saint also accomplished what Nelson (2017) notes as important in the program she studied for Mexican American youth in middle school by embedding an after-school program within the school. Saint was both a school and an after-school program in one, keeping students occupied during the full day as well as for much of the summer. Over time the school has also diversified its after-school options so students can participate in chosen sports, yearbook, dance, or other activities that are givens for their wealthier peers (Lareau 2011). But academics and completing homework are still central to the activities that students do after school.

Saint staff also worked hard to transition students to good high schools. They advocated for financial aid for their students and served as brokers between students and high schools. In this way Saint helped to make sure that their graduates had both access and opportunity at more than just their assigned public high school. Saint then stayed with students and their parents long after they graduated, providing information, help with forms, and safe spaces to gather after school. Having a place to go to do homework, get assistance, and meet up with former classmates was particularly important in the first two years of high school, especially if alumni went to a school with different student demographics than Saint. This gave students access to trusted persons with the know-how to help them in their next stage of schooling. It also gave alumni a chance to give back to their school by tutoring and talking with current students about the transition to high school and later college. While students often came back to Saint to help current students, it was also a time when they checked in with Saint staff. Said Danielle about coming back to Saint as part of her community service hours for high school, "A lot of graduates would still come back [to Saint] to do the activity period. And the teachers would always want to know what was going on, how I was doing, how home was, how school was. They would always ask questions."

But the transition to high school was difficult for both the students who attended the "best" high schools and those who did not get into those schools. For some Saint students who attended private high schools, schools became places of doubt and uncertainty and also alienation. Were they good enough to be there? Did they belong with students in this very different world of wealth and status? Saint alumni struggled when they encountered what Castagno (2014) refers to as a system that attempted to "educate them in whiteness" when they enrolled at either a private high school or a selective college. Transitioning to such schools resulted in individual stress and caused some students to leave these institutions. Cox (2017) notes the trade-offs that many students from low-income families face in adjusting to elite boarding schools. While attendance at such schools provides access to valued resources, there are social and emotional costs. Without transitional supports these students are likely to isolate themselves, as Veronica did at her private high school, and are also at risk of dropping out.

For students who attended the public schools, they wondered about their value given how "easy" the coursework was, at least the first year. Students in both cases needed structures of support. Support from teachers, staff, and programs that bring together students "like us" can help mitigate these situations and change the structures of schools. It is also important that schools allow students to continue to have consistent contact with staff at their previously trusted institution. To graduate more students, teachers and advisors need to actively help students in their transitions and to continually certify that they belong on the college track.

Certification of the ability of students to be on the college-going path was important for students through their full educational trajectory. Acceptance into a competitive private school signaled to students and their families their potential. But for the students not accepted there was a hit to their self-esteem and confidence in their academic ability. It felt like a form of failure and disappointment for those who did not get into one of the coveted private high schools. On the other hand, by going to Saint students were overprepared for their assigned public high schools, and many lost interest in academics and instead spent time with peers who were not on the college track. The charter high school, which is now in the neighborhood, provided an alternative, and its similar size, structure, and demographics to Saint helped more students stay on track.

Schools also needed to not give up on students (Shalaby 2017). Patty persisted and stayed on the college-going path even though discouraged when not supported by Saint in applying to a private high school. She found her inner drive and ultimately those who believed in her at her charter high school, "My freshman year I didn't do so well, I was like I'm done with school after middle school. I HATED school. I didn't even want to try. But my sophomore year, I honestly don't know what it was, I just looked at my family, my parents were born in Mexico and I come from a low-income family, my brother dropped out of college and I was kind of like 'someone has to do it.' All these people are telling me I can't do it, that doesn't define me." Patty then joined sports teams and made the honor roll every semester after that, eventually developing strong relationships with the vice-principal and her math teacher who helped her apply to college. Even though her adjustment to college was also difficult, Patty found that reminding herself of why she was on the college track kept her going through the difficult periods: "I have to do this for my family and for the people that I know, and for people who don't get a fair chance."

Private Schools and Issues of School Choice

Of course there are criticisms that could be levied against Saint as a private school. Private schools have few restrictions in terms of accountability for the students they educate and their outcomes. They can design their own admissions standards and are often accused of selecting the students most likely to do well. In contrast, by law charter schools cannot handpick students but must select using a lottery system. But unlike traditional public schools, they do not have to take students midyear and have been criticized for not providing adequate resources for students with disabilities or other needs (Darling-Hammond and Lieberman 2012). Depending on which entity sponsors the charter school (district, county, or state), reporting requirements differ.

Many are wary of religious schools, and private schools are often pitted against public schools, with claims made that any resourcing or support of private schools comes at the detriment of a commitment to public schools (Meier and Gasoi 2017). In the short term at least, we can learn from the success of private schools, especially those that work with immigrant communities, at the same time that we maximize the resourcing of public schools. Given the number of students in our education systems, and the need for more students to be prepared for postsecondary schooling, public schools are paramount. There is no way that school choice models that provide vouchers for parents to "spend" at any type of school could offer enough supply to meet the demand. Public schools must be resourced appropriately. And we cannot "pile on" more responsibilities so schools are also expected to make up for the lack of public supports to address poverty and other social issues. Further, despite rhetoric that claims that "choice" is about what parents want, the reality is that public funding of private schools gives the power to the schools, rather than the parents and students. Ultimately private schools choose students, not the other way around. Still, there are things to learn from Catholic schools, especially those that serve immigrant communities. Schools that have the freedom to design structures that first-generation students need can inform the future restructuring of educational pathways.

Catholic schools in particular can be instructive for three main reasons. First, Catholic schools have a long history of educating new immigrants and their children (Bryk, Lee, and Holland 1993; National Council of Catholic Bishops [NCCB] 2000; Thelin 2004) and have played a part in the economic mobility of previous generations of Catholic immigrants (Keister 2007). Second, for many new immigrants, religion is still an important institution and one that is often trusted over government and other social institutions (Carnes 2017; Portes and Rumbaut 2006). Third, Catholic schools have shown a willingness to create schools where most needed, often in communities with no schools or where public schools are severely underfunded. These schools have shown results in helping students get quality educations and enroll in college (Goyette 2014; McCloskey 2011; Wirth 2007). Catholics have access to economic as well as social capital. Further, a cultural teaching of the religion is of supporting structures for equality. Those who have created new Catholic schools for students from families with low incomes have been able to harness this history and current resources to build new schools and networks of schools (Katsouros 2017; Kearney 2008; Wirth 2007). For example, in the mid-1990s the first Cristo Rey high school was formed in Chicago. This network of high schools serves similar populations of students as do the Nativity middle schools.

College

To increase the enrollment of underrepresented students in college, many outreach programs that work with students while in middle and high school have assumed a three-stage process to get and keep students on the college path: predisposition to college, information about institutions and the application process, and choice when students select one school to attend (Hossler and Gallagher 1987). This model suggests that the college path is a linear one, with one stage building on the previous. Following this model alone is ineffective for first-generation college students. Students who are members of transitional generations require more, as the students profiled in this book have shown. There is a constant need for reaffirmation of students' ability to be on the college path and certification throughout their educational trajectory, especially when transitioning to different schools. Further, we saw that FGC students are very likely to change their college, with high school counselors assuming one choice and students ultimately choosing a different college (and often one that undermatches their ability) because of family or financial considerations.

It cannot be overlooked that family wealth (distinct from family income) is a factor in predicting students' likelihood of enrolling in and completing college (Conley 2001). Thus, the work of colleges in equalizing the college experience and granting of degrees for all students will not be easy as long as parents with more resources hoard those assets (Hamilton, Roksa, and Nielsen 2018). Colleges therefore need to provide programs and outreach for students least likely to have the same types of parental support. This is particularly difficult because most FGC students go to colleges that have the fewest resources to provide such interventions. Thus, policy makers at the state and federal levels as well as foundations and wealthy individuals who typically donate to private institutions could think about what it would take to move this funding instead to public colleges, perhaps even those institutions that serve the most first-generation college students. And selective colleges would do well to look at their data about the percentage of their students who are low income and are FGC and ask what else they can do to be more accessible to these students (Contreras 2016; Nichols 2017).

At the school level, Yesenia recommends that schools provide "groups for the various things that young people need. You know, social, academics, health and wellness, and another to help you explore your future. And then in high school, look at a student as a whole person, not just the academic side, make sure they are okay." Nunn (2018) provides guidelines for the role that college faculty can play in helping FGC and first-year students transition to college and believe in their ability to do well.

Finally, Perna, Cooper, and Li (2010) note that school administrators need to also understand how much their students must work to pay for their expenses and realize its effects on academic outcomes. Colleges can become places that help students make decisions about what kind of work can best help them balance school and their economic situation.

The Role of Policy

At a time when even parents with high incomes fear for the well-being of their children in the college admissions and degree completion process (Cooper 2014; Hamilton 2016), parents are doing everything they can to offer their own children an advantage. And as tuition at both public and private colleges continues to rise, middle-income families, including parents with resources and abilities to navigate higher education for their children, are increasingly looking to public state and community colleges as options (Sallie Mae 2018). This comes with the risk that the advantages of human, social, and cultural capital that come with those families will further disadvantage first-generation and other students who do not have such resources.

One finding of this study is realizing that enrolling in the best high schools and being academically gifted and motivated are not enough to keep first-generation college students solidly on the path to a college degree. One of the major strategies of Saint to "break the cycle of poverty via education" was to get students into the private Catholic high schools where the expected next step was enrollment in a four-year college. While attending a private high school was predictive of ultimately enrolling in a four-year college, it could not counteract the pull that poverty had on students and their families when economic survival had to be the first priority. As Goldrick-Rab (2018) notes, "Higher education neglects Abraham Maslow's lessons at its peril. Without their basic needs secured, large numbers of today's undergraduates are struggling to learn. Sleepless nights and empty stomachs distract them from going to class and passing their courses, prolonging or even preventing degree completion. Food and housing insecurity are not the personal problems of a few low-income or first-generation students. They stem from systemic failures of both policy and practice and affect millions."

Recent surveys at colleges and universities around the country indicate that at least one-third of students at bachelor's-degree-granting institutions and between 40 and 50 percent of community college students are dealing with food and/or housing insecurity (Hope Lab 2018). When Saint alumni finished high school and turned eighteen, they did not turn their backs on the economic needs of their families. The effects of poverty and a lack of a sustained macro-level response to growing up in a low-income family affect all levels of students' lives and their ultimate success in education. Students need a stable economic situation in which to learn, and so do their families. Even for those students who make it to the middle class, the economic and social support needs of their kin will continue to pull on them, risking their ability to stay in the middle class and reduce their ability to save for the college tuitions of their own children (Vallejo 2012).

State-level Promise Programs are providing some inroads to making tuition more affordable at public institutions. While this helps with enrollment, state colleges also need more funding to provide for the advising needs of students as well as for academic support. Further, at the federal level there needs to be an initiative to incentivize the investment of private wealth into public institutions (Gladwell n.d.). Goldrick-Rab (2016), in *Paying the Price*, lays out very specific suggestions for how financial aid and tuition need to be restructured so more students can go to college and ultimately graduate.

The assistance offered to students transitioning between two- and four-year schools must also be improved. Recent work by the California Community College Chancellor's Office has resulted in agreements to accept students with associate's degrees at more four-year public and private schools, necessary if the state is to increase its dismal rate of successful transfers (Association of Independent California Colleges and Universities [AICCU] 2018). For this to be effective, attention must be paid to the transition of students between schools, especially for students currently on the meandering and dead-end path.

In addition, at both the school and state levels more needs to be done to help students reduce the need for them to work a large number of hours while also going to college. Perna, Cooper, and Li (2010) suggest greater financial support to individuals and also for policies that support colleges that serve a large number of working students. They also recommend that colleges create a campus culture that supports the needs of working students.

Finally, although not a panacea for the faulty immigration system the United States has perpetuated for years, DACA has allowed paths of mobility for students who are undocumented. Although they are not eligible for federal financial aid, receiving DACA allowed students to work legally, which was a huge relief and form of support for students and their families, and allowed them to also stay in school (Silver 2018). With DACA students could work on or off campus, receive stipends to be resident advisors or help with orientation, be part of club leadership, and other activities that previously limited students because of their status (Nichols and Guzmán 2017). DACA also exposed the different realities faced by students depending on the state that they lived in (Nichols 2019; Silver 2018). For Saint alumni, staying in California, which provided the opportunity to apply for in-state tuition and state financial aid, was instrumental. Students also hoped that the promises made by city and county officials to be areas of sanctuary could protect their parents, other family members, and neighborhood from the mass deportations being threatened in some communities.

For Current Students

Structural fixes at the organizational, neighborhood, and policy levels will take time. In the short term, there are ways that readers can use the insights revealed by the students in this book to increase their own success in college.

At the individual level, students need to continue to do well in school, work hard, and be determined to fight through barriers to access good schools and opportunities. As Ward (2000; 2018) notes, students must channel their resistance and resilience when they feel marginalized in educational institutions. She defines resistance as "the ability to recognize and resist negative social influences . . . including learning to stand up against those who dare to limit who or what you choose to be" (Ward 2018, 13) and resilience as "a process in which people dynamically and positively adapt within the context of adversity" (Luthar and Cicchetti 2000, cited by Ward 2018, 13).

It is not fair that only some students have to deal with adversity and counter negative assessments of their abilities, in a system that is not set up for them to succeed. When students cannot reach the traditional path to college, they often blame themselves. We cannot expect students to go it alone given this reality at this point in our history.

Ali, who was successful in staying on the traditional college path, defined her success as a combination of factors and noted the inordinate amount of determination and ability she needed to "push through" barriers: "Well, I

think what contributed to me getting to where I am today, it's partly determination and I think there were a lot of people that kept telling me that I
couldn't do it and that I was like dreaming too much and part of it was I
wanted to prove them wrong and show them that I could do it and my
options weren't limited." Individual drive combined with support, access,
and opportunity allowed some Saint students like Ali to persist past the barriers. The barriers point to the places where larger structural forces need to
change so student success is not so dependent on only the few students with
the combination of determination and necessary resources to persist.

The experiences of the students profiled in this book point to a multi-
tude of advice for all students on the path to college, especially those who
will be the first in their families to pursue education or certain careers. The
first piece of advice is to find people with know-how who both understand
students' abilities as well as help them navigate multiple school transitions.
These might be located in formal programs or mentors from schools or neighborhoods. Another resource for students is to enroll in summer bridge
programs or other kinds of support groups once they are at a new school.
And if classes are too easy, students need to proactively seek more challenging options. Finally, good advisors are key to getting through college. If
feeling down or discouraged, students need to seek support. Teachers and
school staff need to communicate, and students need to believe, that one
bad grade or struggling in a course does not mean a student is a failure or not
"cut out" for college. Students need encouragement to visit faculty during
their office hours, ask for help, and find others who are trustworthy.

It is also useful for students and their advisors to remember that transitions between schools are potentially vulnerable times and extra support
may be necessary. For example, Langenkamp (2011) found that for middle
school students who are socially isolated, staying with people they know
when transitioning to high school results in better outcomes than going to
a high school where they do not know anyone.

Patty, who felt very out of place at her college away from home, said that
the experience of being on a very white campus with wealthy roommates

made my pride in my culture, stronger. At first I felt so different and I just
wanted to hide it away, but throughout the year I learned to embrace my
culture and be who I was. When I brought my Mexico flag and I hung it on
my wall, that was my reminder every day. I don't think any of my roommates
saw it that way, but it was my way of saying this is who I am and let the world

see it. I told myself, at the end of the day they can say what they want, but this is for my family and this is for me.

Her advice for other first-generation students who feel similar in their school environment is to

> be who you are and embrace your culture. And if someone thinks that you are different, you know, being different is good, it's not a bad thing. And I think like the most important thing is that, if you feel alone, if you feel just kinda separated from everyone else, talk to someone. I excluded myself from everyone and I was by myself for a long time, I felt like I kinda got depressed, I suffered a lot of anxiety while I was [at college], and me not talking to anyone made it worse. Be mentally prepared because I didn't think it was going to hit me as hard as it did. So, to be prepared that culture shock is real and to just be aware.

First-generation college students who graduate need to also remember that when *they* have children they will likely not have the resources of those parents who are the second generation or more who have gone to college (Lawrence 2016). Seeking out additional resources is important especially for those who want to attend a highly selective college. As Yesenia remarked, "First-generations do need an extra push. Because their families don't know what it's like to go through college, to go through all this. So, someone outside of that, kind of, who knows that they're capable of going to college, encouraging them."

Students who struggled and stayed on the college path maintained relationships with the people who first believed in them. They did not give up or succumb to shame if things were not working out or they were told no. They kept asking until they found people who understood and were willing to help. Martín's advice was this: "I have friends and my neighbors and they barely graduated high school and I tell them, whoa, take advantage of your parents for sure. Take advantage because when you're living in you're not paying rent. Just take advantage of the whole situation, work on yourself, work on your money, on your career, go to school while you can because if you're living alone and you're paying rent and trying to go to school you can't. It's really, really hard. But if you have your parents and you have schools around. Take advantage of the situation definitely."

Educational Paths and Transitions: Taking the Long Journey

Focusing on the educational journeys of transitional generations and engaging in the hard work of structural change will take bold leadership. Those who are born into a family where both their grandparents and parents graduated from college have the highest overall family incomes (Lawrence 2016). Increasing the proportion of the U.S. population who are continuing-generation college students provides the very high likelihood that enough time has passed for such families to acquire the wealth needed to pay for college. But to get to that point more must be done to get FGC students through college. We must move beyond the structural limitations of our school silos and provide opportunities for students to link lives in ways that support them in all their school transitions and through their full educational trajectories.

Changes to the education system alone will not provide better outcomes for students. Without attention to family economic issues and stability, social mobility via education will be an unrealized dream for many FGC students (Mullen 2010). It will take collective work, or what Dixon-Román (2017) refers to as "enabling possibilities," to embrace this societal journey, and transition more families in the United States to college-going families. And we must do this without putting all the pressure on first-generation college students to go it alone. Although our systems will need to change and more resources be provided, the effort is worth it to move our society to one with a more educated citizenry. And the first-generation students who were profiled in this book can help us get there.

Appendix

●

Methodology and Researcher Positionality

The data in this study come from multiple sources, including interviews and analysis of secondary data sets. Observations at Saint Middle School and in the neighborhood took place mainly during the 2017–2018 school year. I also analyzed existing public datasets on the schools that Saint students attended as well as census and other neighborhood and national data when appropriate. Names of students and schools, including Saint Middle, have been changed. My observations at Saint were limited to the graduate support room; I did not interact with current students. In two cases occupational information about interviewees or their parents has been changed to reduce the likelihood of identifying the alumni.

Data on Saint Alumni

I conducted fifty-one interviews with alumni from Saint Middle School. To contact potential interviewees, the full population of Saint alumni who graduated eighth grade over a four-year period and were now in their early twenties as well as a cohort who were sophomores in high school were contacted by the graduate support director at Saint. Alumni were sent emails and texted multiple times throughout the year of the research study. In addition, three students were referred by other interviewees. The bulk of the qualitative data included in this book are from the interviews with forty-two students who graduated as eighth-graders from Saint and were young adults. Nine interviews were conducted with Saint alumni when they were in high school. The purpose of these interviews was to verify the recollections of older Saint alumni as to their transition from middle to high school and their assessments of what they liked and disliked about Saint. Although the high school students were few in number, they served to confirm that Saint alumni who graduated earlier had similar memories and experiences transitioning from middle to high school.

Interviews took place at Saint, in public libraries, at colleges where students were currently attending, or in their homes; if students were away at school and not on break, I interviewed them by phone. The conversations lasted one to two hours. Interviewees were provided with a gift card of their choice as a thank-you for their time.

All interviews were recorded, transcribed, and coded for main themes. Initial analysis revealed five paths that students took post–high school, and further analysis was done of the experiences of students within each path. Then a higher order analysis was done to determine themes across all five paths (the basis of the content in chapter 5).

In addition, analyses were conducted on quantitative data from the full population of all Saint alumni who graduated since the school started (class of 2004 through class of 2017). The deidentified data provide information about year of graduation from Saint, elementary and high schools attended, any postsecondary schools attended, as well as other activities such as working or military service. The data are updated each spring by staff at Saint. I used data from the last available update in the spring of 2017. In table 2.2 I analyze the trajectories of alumni for all the graduates ($N = 245$), but in other analyses where I compare the full population to Saint alumni I interviewed, I restrict the analysis to only those who graduated in the same four years as the interview cohorts ($n = 154$). Table A.1 compares the characteristics of the full population of Saint alumni who graduated eighth grade in the same period to those of the sample of interviewees. This provides an opportunity to see where overrepresentation occurred depending on who volunteered to be interviewed. Ultimately, I interviewed 27 percent of the population of alumni who graduated from Saint in the four-year period.

Table A.1
Comparing Population of Saint Graduates to Interviewees

	Population of Saint Alum Four Cohorts (*N* = 154) (%)	Saint Interviewees (*n* = 42) (%)
All students:		
Attended public elementary school	99	100
Attended private high school	54	69
Attended public high school	29	19
Attended charter high school	17	12
Of those enrolled in postsecondary:		
Enrolled in 4-year public college	41	45
Enrolled in 4-year private college	19	26
Enrolled in 2-year public college	37	24
Enrolled in for-profit or trade school	3	5

My write-up and analyses were shared with the five students profiled in the book for feedback. Students corrected minor errors and commented on the tone and analysis and expressed any concerns they had about identifying information, which I subsequently addressed. All interviewees were updated as the research project progressed, and I met with any who wanted to know more about the results. I also periodically updated the staff at Saint about my findings. I shared the findings with the director of graduate support and two administrators to see if the patterns I was noticing matched their own observations of alumni outcomes. I also made myself available to help with any other research needs of the school. In this capacity I ran separate analyses of surveys Saint had conducted with parents and provided tables and charts as well as a literature review. These they used for their own internal purposes.

Secondary School, Neighborhood, and National Data

I also analyzed school and neighborhood data from datasets publicly available from the College Scorecard, the American Fact Finder, and the U.S. Census Bureau. Data from the California Department of Education provided information about both public and, when available, private schools attended by the interviewees. I also ran descriptive analyses using nationally representative public-use data from the National Education Longitudinal Study of 2002 through 2012.

Limitations of the Research

While a benefit of this study is that it starts with aspiring FGC students' educational experiences sooner than high school, it is limited in that it begins with students who attended the same middle school. This can be seen as a positive as well as a negative. On the positive side, by limiting the school I am controlling for students who had a similar middle school experience and thus can examine differentiation within the similar context. Further, many of the students came from the same neighborhood, which also helps control for differences at the exo level. On the negative side, there are many selection effects because the findings are tied to students who were accepted to the private school. To partially address this limitation, secondary data on students nationally are included to give readers perspective on how Saint students compare to FGC Latina/o students nationally.

It is also important for me to acknowledge that I did not interview any teachers or college counselors beyond my discussions with the graduate support director and administrators at Saint. The perspectives presented in this book are those of the students and their perceptions and recollections of their experiences in the schools they attended.

Limitations of the Researcher

The question of researchers being insiders or outsiders needs to be addressed in this study. As a white, U.S.-born, European American adult who speaks limited Spanish, I am clearly an outsider in the community in which this study took place. Although I have spent time and have worked in the community, in different capacities, for over ten years and even tutored students in an after-school program long ago in the building where Saint is now located, I have never lived in the community, nor have I ever taught in K–12 schools.

To help compensate for my language deficiencies, I had a student research assistant who is bilingual in Spanish and English conduct one interview with a high school student. She passed the ethics course for research with human subjects, translated interview and consent forms into Spanish, and was trained in the interview guide and about the overall study. She was available if any parents had questions about the research.

I also want to take a moment to address the approach I took writing this book. Students whom I interviewed, on all of the paths, were very optimistic about their futures. In her study of students taking different paths to college, Ovink (2017) found herself being more critical than the students about the paths they were taking and what that meant for their futures. Similarly, in this study all but a few students were very positive about their experience at Saint as well as at their high schools. Overall students were appreciative of the opportunity to attend Saint and any private schools to which they received scholarships. I think I mirrored this optimism in my approach to the data, the write up of findings, and in the tone of this book. But there were two students who were critical of Saint and the private high schools they attended. Although I did talk about the experiences of students who were critical of their schools, I did not make that the focus of my analysis.

Acknowledgments

My immense gratitude goes to those who talked with me about their educational journeys. I am grateful to them as well as to their families for their openness. Thank you to the staff at Saint Middle School who helped me contact alumni, were very open to the findings, read the draft manuscript, and responded to my questions.

Thank you to colleagues and friends who gave me valuable feedback at different stages of the proposal and project, some of whom read portions or even all of the text, including Terri Peretti, Alma García, Anna Sampaio, Jennifer Ng, Christy Castle, Michelle Myers, Jesica Fernández, and Alma Orozco. Thank you to Veronica Marquez who helped with the initial stages of data collection as a student research assistant.

Thank you to the members of the Sociology Department at Santa Clara University (SCU) and our chair Enrique Pumar for supporting research and teaching. Thank you also to the members of two faculty writing groups who have provided support throughout this whole project: Barbara, Naomi, Pat, Jennifer, and Kristi.

The Ignatian Center for Jesuit Education at Santa Clara University provided funding for this project. I thank especially Theresa Ladrigan-Whelpley who envisioned the Common Good Faculty Collaborative and the members of the Economic Justice group that commented on my research project proposals. I also thank the Office of the Provost, the Office of Faculty Development, and the University Research Committee at SCU. This project could not have been completed without Santa Clara University's generous sabbatical policy as well as support for research including financial assistance for indexing and a course release.

Thank you to those at Rutgers University Press for all the work they do to publish research in the social sciences, especially in the area of education. I am most appreciative to Lisa Banning for her guidance, expertise, and timely work at all stages of the project as well as Cheryl Hirsch and Joseph Dahm at the production stage.

The book benefited from the comments of anonymous reviewers both at the proposal and in the final stages. I am indebted to them for their careful reading and suggestions. Thank you to Lisa Nunn who has written about first-generation college students and is the editor of the Critical Issues in American Education series at Rutgers. Thank you also to the scholars cited here, especially those who have focused their attention on the experiences of first-generation college students and those who are committed to producing research to change our education systems to make them work more effectively for all students.

And thank you to my friends and family for supporting me, especially John and Niamh for their encouragement, love, and support, and for giving me the space and time to devote to this project.

Notes

Introduction

1   All school and student names are pseudonyms.
2   Based on data for 2016. See https://datacenter.kidscount.org to get updated statistics by year.

Chapter 1   Paths Diverged

1   In 2017 about 66 percent of adults age twenty-five and older in the United States had less than a bachelor's degree. See https://nces.ed.gov/programs/digest/d17/tables/dt17_104.10.asp?current=yes.
2   It is important to note that a recession occurred in the United States during the period when this study took place. Research by Cozzolino, Smith, and Crosnoe (2018) shows that the recession affected college-aged students differently depending on social class, with those of higher classes less likely to experience a disruption in degree completion.
3   Throughout this book "Latino" and "Latina" are used interchangeably.
4   The California Poverty Measure (CPM) is a new index that improves upon conventional poverty measures. The CPM tracks necessary expenditures, adjusts for geographic differences in housing costs, and includes food stamps and other noncash benefits as resources available to poor families. See www.inequality.stanford.edu/cpm.
5   See https://aspe.hhs.gov/poverty-guidelines to get the latest poverty figures and read more about how the poverty line is calculated at the federal level.

Chapter 2   Being a Transitional Generation and Navigating Schools

1   For more information about the different types of generations by education, see Lawrence (2016).

2 There is no official body that defines or names generations; usually a term emerges in the press and then is picked up and used by others. See www.pewresearch.org /fact-tank/2018/03/01/defining-generations-where-millennials-end-and-post -millennials-begin/.

3 For the purposes of this project I use the same definition of FGC as the National Center for Education Statistics: a first-generation college student is a student for whom both parents have a high school degree or less (Chen and Carroll 2005; Choy 2001). For analyses of national data, the outcomes of FGC students are compared to those of two other groups by parents' educational background: students for whom at least one parent has some college (SC), which could include those who have received an associate's degree or vocational or technical certificate as well as those who attended a four-year college but never received a bachelor's degree. Usually FGC and SC students are compared to students in the continuing generation college (CGC) group, or those for whom at least one parent has a minimum of a bachelor's degree.

4 See Kleinberg (2006) and Brown and McKeown (1997) for more information about how religious organizations provided cash assistance to mothers widowed because of war, support that was then adopted as social policy first by individual states and then by the federal government, becoming the system that is known as welfare today.

5 Police chiefs and officers who work in cities with large populations of undocu-mented immigrants know that public safety, for citizen and noncitizen residents, can be compromised if people are afraid to talk to the police (Smart 2018).

6 A very small number of students from Saint who were high school sophomores at the time of the study are included in chapter 3 about transitions from middle to high school. See the method section in the appendix for more information about these students and the overall research design and sample.

7 In this book I use the terms "transition to adulthood" and "emerging adults" even though Arnett (2015, 23, emphases original) prefers the term "emerging adult-hood" to "transition to adulthood" to refer to those in their late teens and twenties. He writes, "One problem of thinking of the years from the late teens through the twenties as merely the transition to adulthood leads to a focus on what young people in that age period are *becoming*, at the cost of neglecting what they *are*." In this book, examining many different types of transitions, the focus is on the mechanisms and processes that young adults engage as they make these transitions during a particular time in their lives.

8 For example, see *Paying for the Party* by Elizabeth Armstrong and Laura Hamil-ton (2013) and *Class and Campus Life* by Elizabeth Lee (2016). Check out *Degrees of Inequality* by Ann Mullen (2010) or *Inside the College Gates: How Class and Culture Matter in Higher Education* by Jenny Stuber (2011).

9 There is also a film that shows the trajectories of FGC students at the end of their high school years. See www.youtube.com/watch?v=pfDx4duheHk.

10 Even though I am looking at students earlier in their educational trajectories and therefore include individuals that studies that start at high school or college might exclude, this study still misses students who never attended the middle school I call Saint. The selection effects of this are exacerbated because Saint is a private school: students who applied but were not accepted are not included in this study. I talk about all these limitations further in the appendix.

11 Nativity schools are solely middle schools. The Cristo Rey network is a similar model that focuses on high schools. These schools operate independently from one another.

Chapter 3   Middle and High School Transitions and Experiences on the Path to College

1 Since the administration realized that not having such activities put students at a disadvantage in being able to join sports and activities in high school, Saint now does have sports teams that compete against those from other private Catholic middle schools as well as clubs and activities after school.

2 For guidelines on filing the FAFSA form for parents who are undocumented, see https://studentaid.ed.gov/sa/sites/default/files/financial-aid-and-undocumented -students.pdf.

References

Adachi, Fugi F. 1979. "Analysis of the First-Generation College Student Population: A New Concept in Higher Education." Unpublished manuscript. Laramie: University of Wyoming Division of Student Educational Opportunity.

Alexander, Karl, Doris Entwisle, and Linda Olson. 2014. *The Long Shadow: Family Background, Disadvantaged Urban Youth, and the Transition to Adulthood.* New York: Russell Sage Foundation.

Alon, Sigal, and Marta Tienda. 2005. "Assessing the 'Mismatch' Hypothesis: Differentials in College Graduation Rates by Institutional Selectivity." *Sociology of Education* 78(4):294–315.

Alvarado, Steven Elias. 2016. "Delayed Disadvantage: Neighborhood Context and Child Development." *Social Forces* 94(4):1847–1877.

Amato, Paul R. 2005. "The Impact of Family Formation Change on the Cognitive, Social, and Emotional Well-Being of the Next Generation." *The Future of Children* 15(2):75–96.

Anderson, Nick. 2017. "More Colleges to Add Lower-Income Students." *San Jose Mercury News.* December 24, 2017.

Armstrong, Elizabeth, and Laura Hamilton. 2013. *Paying for the Party: How College Maintains Inequality.* Cambridge, MA: Harvard University Press.

Arnett, Jeffrey Jensen. 2015. *Emerging Adulthood: The Winding Road from the Late Teens Through the Twenties.* Oxford: Oxford University Press.

Association of Independent California Colleges and Universities (AICCU). 2018. "New California Community Colleges Agreement with Private Colleges and Universities Marks Major Expansion of Associate Degree for Transfer Program." July 25, 2018. www.aiccu.edu/2018/07/25/new-california-community-colleges -agreement-aiccu- marks-major-expansion-associate-degree-transfer-program/.

Atherton, Matthew C. 2014. "Academic Preparedness of First-Generation College Students: Different Perspectives." *Journal of College Student Development* 55(8):824–829.

Auerbach, Susan. 2004. "Engaging Latino Parents in Supporting College Pathways: Lessons from a College Access Program." *Journal of Hispanic Higher Education* 3(2):125–145.

Bailey, Thomas, Davis Jenkins, Clive Belfield, and Elizabeth Kopko. 2016. *Matching Talents to Careers: From Self-Directed to Guided Pathways*. Cambridge, MA: Harvard Education Press.

Beattie, Irenee R. 2018. "Sociological Perspectives on First Generation College Students." In *The Handbook of Sociology of Education for the 21st Century*, edited by Barbara Schneider, 171–191. New York: Springer.

Beattie, Irenee R., and Megan Thiele. 2015. "Connecting in Class? College Class Size and Inequality in Academic Social Capital." *Journal of Higher Education* 87(3):332–362.

Benner, Aprile D., Alaina E. Boyle, and Sydney Sadler. 2016. "Parental Involvement and Adolescents' Educational Success: The Roles of Prior Achievement and Socioeconomic Status." *Journal of Youth and Adolescence* 45:1053–1064.

Berman, Jillian. 2018. "There's a Growing Need for Child-Care Centers on College Campuses." *Market Watch*. June 9, 2018. www.marketwatch.com/story/the-fate-of -thousands- of-college-students-and-their-kids-hangs-in-the-balance-2018-06-04.

Billson, Janet Mancini, and Margaret Brooks Terry. 1982. "In Search of the Silken Purse: Factors in Attrition among First-Generation Students." *College and University* 58:57–75.

Bjorklund-Young, Alanna. 2016. "Family Income and the College Completion Gap." Johns Hopkins School of Education, Institute for Education Policy. March 2016. http://edpolicy.education.jhu.edu/wp-content/uploads/2016/03/Familyincomean dcollegegapmastheadFINAL.pdf.

Bronfenbrenner, Urie. 1979. *The Ecology of Human Development: Experiments by Nature and Design*. Cambridge, MA: Harvard University Press.

Brown, Dorothy M., and Elizabeth McKeown. 1997. *The Poor Belong to Us: Catholic Charities and American Welfare*. Cambridge, MA: Harvard University Press.

Bryk, Anthony S., Valerie E. Lee, and Peter B. Holland. 1993. *Catholic Schools and the Common Good*. Cambridge, MA: Harvard University Press.

Bureau of Labor Statistics. 2013. "Current Population Survey."

Cahalan, Margaret, Laura Perna, Mika Yamashita, Roman Ruiz, and Khadish Franklin. 2016. "Indicators of Higher Education Equity in the United States: 2016 Historical Trend Report." Washington, DC: Pell Institute for the Study of Opportunity in Higher Education, Council for Opportunity in Education, and Alliance for Higher Education and Democracy of the University of Pennsylvania.

Calarco, Jessica McCrory. 2018. *Negotiating Opportunities: How the Middle Class Secures Advantages in School*. Oxford: Oxford University Press.

Carnes, Michael M. 2017. "Alma Mater, Mater Exulum, Jesuit Education and Immigration in America: A Moral Framework Rooted in History and Mission." In *Undocumented and in College: Students and Institutions in a Climate of National Hostility*, edited by Terry-Ann Jones and Laura Nichols, 84–103. New York: Fordham University Press.

Carnevale, Anthony P., and Nicole Smith. 2018. *Balancing Work and Learning: Implications for Low-Income Students*. Georgetown University, Center on Education and the Workforce.

Carnevale, Anthony P., Nicole Smith, and Jeff Strohl. 2014. *Recovery: Job Growth and Education Requirements through 2020*. Georgetown University, Center on Education and the Workforce.

Carnevale, Anthony P., and Jeff Strohl. 2010. "How Increasing College Access Is Increasing Inequality, and What to Do about It." In *Rewarding Strivers: Helping Low-Income Students Succeed in College*, edited by R. D. Kahlenberg, 71–190. New York: Century Foundation Press.

Castagno, Angelina E. 2014. *Educated in Whiteness: Good Intentions and Diversity in Schools*. Minneapolis: University of Minnesota Press.

Castleman, Benjamin L., and Lindsay C. Page. 2013. "A Trickle or a Torrent? Understanding the Extent of Summer 'Melt' among College-Intending High School Graduates." *Social Science Quarterly* 95(1):202–220.

Cataldi, Emily Forrest, Christopher T. Bennett, and Xianglei Chen. 2018. "First- Generation Students: College Access, Persistence, and Post Bachelor's Outcomes." Stats in Brief, NCES 2018-421. National Center for Education Statistics. February 2018.

Ceja, Miguel. 2006. "Understanding the Role of Parents and Siblings as Information Sources in the College Choice Process of Chicana Students." *Journal of College Student Development* 47(1):87–104.

Center for Applied Research in the Apostolate (CARA). 2016. "Frequently Requested Church Statistics." http://cara.georgetown.edu/frequently-requested-church -statistics/.

Center for Research on Education Outcomes (CREDO). 2015. "Urban Charter School Study Report on 41 Regions." http://urbancharters.stanford.edu/download /Urban%20Charter%20School%20Study%20Report%20on%2041%20Regions.pdf.

Center on Budget and Policy Priorities. 2017. "Pell Grants—a Key Tool for Expanding College Access and Economic Opportunity—Need Strengthening, Not Cuts." July 27, 2017. www.cbpp.org/research/federal-budget/pell-grants-a-key-tool-for -expanding- college-access-and-economic-opportunity.

Chen, Xianglei, and C. Dennis Carroll. 2005. "First-Generation Students in Postsecondary Education: A Look at Their College Transcripts." U.S. Department of Education, Institute of Education Sciences.

Chetty, Raj, John N. Friedman, Emmanuel Saez, Nicholas Turner, and Danny Yagan. 2017. "Mobility Report Cards: The Role of Colleges in Intergenerational Mobility." January 2017. www.equality-of-opportunity.org/papers/coll_mrc_paper.pdf.

Chingos, Matthew, and Daniel Kuehn. 2017. "The Effects of Statewide Private School Choice on College Enrollment and Graduation." Urban Institute. September 27, 2017.

Choy, Susan. 2001. "Students Whose Parents Did Not Go to College: Postsecondary Access, Persistence, and Attainment." National Center for Education Statistics.

College Equity Report. 2018. Indiana Commission for Higher Education. www.in.gov /che/files/2018_College_Equity_Report.PDF.

Collier, Peter J., and David L. Morgan. 2008. "Is That Paper Really Due Today?" Differences in First-Generation and Traditional College Students' Understandings of Faculty Expectations." *Higher Education* 55(4):425–446.

Conley, Dalton. 2001. "Capital for College: Parental Assets and Postsecondary Schooling." *Sociology of Education* 74:59–72.

Contreras, Frances. 2016. "Latino Students in Catholic Postsecondary Institutions." *Journal of Catholic Education* 19(2):81–111.

Cooper, Catherine R. 2014. "Cultural Brokers: How Immigrant Youth in Multicultural Societies Navigate and Negotiate Their Pathways to College Identities." *Learning, Culture and Social Interaction* 3:170–176.

Cottom, Tressie McMillan. 2017. *Lower Ed: The Troubling Rise of For-Profit Colleges in the New Economy*. New York: New Press.

Cox, Amanda Barrett. 2017. "Cohorts, 'Siblings,' and Mentors: Organizational Structures and the Creation of Social Capital." *Sociology of Education* 90(1):47–63.

Cozzolino, Elizabeth, Chelsea Smith, and Robert L. Crosnoe. 2018. "Family-Related Disparities in College Enrollment across the Great Recession." *Sociological Perspectives* 61(5):689–710.

Crosnoe, Robert. 2009. "Low-Income Students and the Socioeconomic Composition of Public High Schools." *American Sociological Review* 74(5):709–730.

Darling-Hammond, Linda, and Ann Lieberman. 2012. "Educating Superman." In *Finding Superman: Debating the Future of Public Education in America*, edited by Watson Scott Swail, 31–45. New York: Teachers College Press.

Davenport, Barbara. 2016. *Grit and Hope: A Year with Five Latino Students and the Program That Helped Them Aim for College*. Berkeley: University of California Press.

Dillon, Eleanor, and Jeffrey Andrew Smith. 2017. "Determinants of the Match between Student Ability and College Quality." *Journal of Labor Economics* 35(11):45–66.

Dixon-Román, Ezekiel J. 2017. *Inheriting Possibility: Social Reproduction and Quantification in Education*. Minneapolis: University of Minnesota Press.

Domina, Thurston, AnneMarie Conley, and George Farkas. 2011. "The Link between Educational Expectations and Effort in the College-for-All Era." *Sociology of Education* 84(2):93–112.

Dorner, Lisa M. 2017. "Turning Points and Tensions." In *Language Brokering in Immigrant Families: Theories and Contexts*, edited by Robert S. Weisskirch, 270–293. New York: Routledge.

Duckworth, Angela. 2016. *Grit: The Power of Passion and Perseverance*. New York: Scribner.

Dumais, Susan A., and Aaryn Ward. 2010. "Cultural Capital and First-Generation College Success." *Poetics* 38(3), 245–265.

Duong, Mylien T., Daryaneh Badaly, Freda F. Liu, David Schwartz, and Carolyn A. McCarty. 2016. "Generational Differences in Academic Achievement among Immigrant Youths: A Meta-analytic Review." *Review of Educational Research* 86(1):3–41.

Eagan, Kevin, Ellen Bara Stolzenberg, Hilary B. Zimmerman, Melissa C. Aragon, Hannah Whang Sayson, and Cecilia Rios-Aguilar. 2017. "The American Freshman: National Norms Fall 2016." Higher Education Research Institute. www.heri.ucla.edu/monographs/TheAmericanFreshman2016.pdf.

Education Trust–West. 2017. "The Majority Report: Supporting the Educational Success of Latino Students in California." https://west.edtrust.org.

Elder, Glen H., Jr. 1985. *Life Course Dynamics: Trajectories, Transitions, 1968–1980*. Ithaca, NY: Cornell University Press.

Engle, Jennifer, and Vincent Tinto. 2008. *Moving beyond Access: College Success for Low-Income, First-Generation Students*. Washington, DC: Pell Institute.

Fallon, Marcia V. 1997. "The School Counselor's Role in First Generation Students' College Plans." *School Counselor* 44:384–393.

Fenzel, L. Mickey. 2009. *Improving Urban Middle Schools: Lessons from the Nativity Schools*. New York: State University of New York Press.

Frenette, Marc. 2006. "Too Far to Go On? Distance to School and University Participation." *Education Economics* 14 (1):31–58.

Frey, Susan. 2012. "California Near Bottom in Number of School Counselors." EdSource. https://edsource.org/2012/california-near-bottom-in-numbers-of-school -counselors/24557.

Galen, Luke W. 2014. "Nonreligious and Atheist Emerging Adults." In *Emerging Adults' Religiousness and Spirituality: Meaning-Making in an Age of Transition*, edited by C. M. Barry and M. M. Abo-Zena, 237–254. Oxford: Oxford University Press.

Gansemer-Topf, Ann M., Jillian Downey, and Ulrike Genschel. 2018. "Overcoming Undermatching: Factors Associated with Degree Attainment for Academically Undermatched Students." *Journal of College Student Retention.* https://doi.org/10 .1177/1521025117753822.

Garza, Alma Nidia, and Andrew S. Fullerton. 2017. "Staying Close or Going Away: How Distance to College Impacts the Educational Attainment and Academic Performance of First-Generation College Students." *Sociological Perspectives* 61(1):164–185.

Ginder, Scott A., Janice E. Kelly-Reid, and Farrah B. Mann. 2017. "Postsecondary Institutions and Cost of Attendance in 2016–17; Degrees and Other Awards Conferred, 2015–16; and 12-Month Enrollment, 2015–16: First Look (Preliminary Data)." NCES 2017-075. U.S. Department of Education, National Center for Education Statistics.

Gladwell, Malcolm. n.d. "My Little Hundred Million." Podcast, Season 1, Episode 6. http://revisionisthistory.com/episodes/06-my-little-hundred-million.

Gofen, Anat. 2009. "Family Capital: How First-Generation Higher Education Students Break the Intergenerational Cycle." *Family Relations* 58(1):104–120.

Goldrick-Rab, Sara. 2006. "Following Their Every Move: An Investigation of Social Class Differences in College Pathways." *Sociology of Education* 79(1):61–79.

———. 2010. "Challenges and Opportunities for Improving Community College Student Success." *Review of Educational Research* 80(3):437–469.

———. 2016. *Paying the Price: College Costs, Financial Aid, and the Betrayal of the American Dream.* Chicago: University of Chicago Press.

———. 2018. "What's the Biggest Challenge for Colleges and Universities?" *New York Times.* June 5, 2018.

Goldrick-Rab, Sara, and Michelle Miller-Adams. 2018. "Don't Dismiss the Value of Free-College Programs. They Do Help Low-Income Students." *Chronicle of Higher Education* 65(3). September 7, 2018.

Gonzales, Roberto G. 2011. "Learning to Be Illegal: Undocumented Youth and Shifting Legal Contexts in the Transition to Adulthood." *American Sociological Review* 76(4):602–619.

———. 2016. *Lives in Limbo: Undocumented and Coming of Age in America.* Berkeley: University of California Press.

Goodchild, Lester F., Richard W. Jonsen, Patty Limerick, and David A. Longanecker, eds. 2014. *Higher Education in the American West.* New York: Palgrave.

Goodman, Joshua, Michael Hurwitz, and Jonathan Smith. 2017. "Access to 4-Year Public Colleges and Degree Completion." *Journal of Labor Economics* 35(3):829–867.

Gordon, Larry. 2018. "They Did It: California Students Who Graduated from State Colleges in Four Years." EdSource. June 3, 2018. https://edsource.org/2018/they-did -it-california-students-who-graduated-from-state- colleges-in-four-years/598347.

Goyette, Kimberly. 2014. "Setting the Context." In *Choosing Homes, Choosing Schools*, edited by A. Lareau and K. Goyette, 1–24. New York: Russell Sage Foundation.

Gramlich, John. 2017. "Hispanic Dropout Rate Hits New Low, College Enrollment at New High." Pew Research Center. September 29, 2017. www.pewresearch.org/fact-tank/2017/09/29/hispanic-dropout-rate-hits-new-low-college-enrollment-at-new-high/.

Granovetter, Mark. 1973. "The Strength of Weak Ties." *American Journal of Sociology* 78:1360–1380.

Hagan, Maria Hagan. 2012. *Migration Miracle: Faith, Hope, and Meaning on the Undocumented Journey*. Cambridge, MA: Harvard University Press.

Hamilton, Laura T. 2016. *Parenting to a Degree: How Family Matters for College Women's Success*. Chicago: University of Chicago Press.

Hamilton, Laura, Josipa Roksa, and Kelly Nielsen. 2018. "Providing a 'Leg Up': Parental Involvement and Opportunity Hoarding in College." *Sociology of Education* 91(2):111–131.

Hao, Lingxin, and Suet-Ling Pong. 2008. "The Role of School in the Upward Mobility of Disadvantaged Immigrants' Children." *Annals of the American Academy* 620:62–89.

Higareda, Ignacio, Shane P. Martin, José M. Chávez, and Karen Holyk-Casey. 2011. "Los Angeles Catholic Schools: Impact and Opportunity for Economically Disadvantaged Students." Los Angeles: Loyola Marymount University.

Hill, Lori Diane. 2008. "School Strategies and the 'College-Linking' Process: Reconsidering the Effects of High Schools on College Enrollment." *Sociology of Education* 81(1):53–76.

Hill, Paul T., Lawrence Angel, and Jon Christensen. 2006. "Charter School Achievement Studies." http://citeseerx.ist.psu.edu/viewdoc/download?doi=10.1.1.466.7085&rep=rep1&type=pdf.

Hillman, Nicholas W. 2016. "Geography of College Opportunity: The Case of Education Deserts." *American Educational Research Journal* 53(4):987–1021.

Holas, Igor, and Aletha C. Huston. 2012. "Are Middle Schools Harmful? The Role of Transition Timing, Classroom Quality and School Characteristics." *Journal of Youth and Adolescence* 41:333–345.

Holland, Megan M. 2019. *Divergent Paths to College: Race, Class, and Inequality in High Schools*. New Brunswick, NJ: Rutgers University Press.

Hope Lab. 2018. "Still Hungry and Homeless in College." https://hope4college.com/still-hungry-and-homeless-in-college/

Hossler, Don, and Karen S. Gallagher. 1987. "Studying Student College Choice: A Three Phase Model and the Implications for Policy Makers." *College and University* 2(3):207–221.

Howell, Jessica S., and Matea Pender. 2015. "The Costs and Benefits of Enrolling in an Academically Matched College." *Economics of Education Review* 51:152–168.

Hoxby, Caroline, and Christopher Avery. 2013. "The Missing 'One-Offs': The Hidden Supply of High Achieving, Low-Income Students." Brookings Papers on Economic Activity.

Huchting, Karen K., Shane P. Martin, José M. Chávez, Karen Holyk-Casey, and Delmy Ruiz. 2014. "Los Angeles Catholic Schools: Academic Excellence and Character Formation for Students Living in Poverty," March 2014. Loyola Marymount University, Center for Catholic Education Research.

Hurtado, Sylvia. 1992. "The Campus Racial Climate: Contexts of Conflict." *Journal of Higher Education* 63(5):539–569.

Hurtado, Sylvia, and Deborah F. Carter 1997. "Effects of College Transition and Perceptions of the Campus Racial Climate on Latino College Students' Sense of Belonging." *Sociology of Education* 70(4):324–345.

Inman, W. Elliot, and Larry Mayes. 1999. "The Importance of Being First: Unique Characteristics of First Generation Community College Students." *Community College Review* 26(3):3–22.

Ishitani, Terry T. 2006. "Studying Attrition and Degree Completion Behavior among First-Generation College Students in the United States." *Journal of Higher Education* 77(5):861–885.

Itzkowitz, Michael. 2018. "New Data Further Cements Completion Crisis in Higher Education." Third Way. February 1, 2018. www.thirdway.org/memo/new-data -further-cements-completion-crisis-in-higher- education.

Jack, Anthony Abraham. 2016. "(No) Harm in Asking: Class, Acquired Cultural Capital, and Academic Engagement at an Elite University." *Sociology of Education* 89(1):1–19.

———. 2019. *The Privileged Poor: How Elite Colleges are Failing Disadvantaged Students*. Cambridge: Harvard University Press.

Jack, Anthony Abraham, and Véronique Irwin. 2018. "Seeking Out Support: Looking beyond Socioeconomic Status to Explain Academic Engagement Strategies at an Elite College." In *Clearing the Path for First- Generation College Students: Qualitative and Intersectional Studies of Educational Mobility*, edited by Ashley C. Rondini, Bedelia Nicola Richards, and Nicolas P. Simon, 135–160. New York: Lexington Books.

Johnson, Hans, Marisol Cuellar Mejia, and Sarah Bohn. 2017. "Will California Run Out of College Graduates?" Public Policy Institute of California. October 2017. www.ppic.org/publication/will-california-run-out-of-college-graduates/.

Justice, Benjamin, and Colin Macleod. 2016. *Have a Little Faith: Religion, Democracy, and the American Public School*. Chicago: University of Chicago Press.

Kalogrides, Demetra. 2009. "Generational Status and Academic Achievement among Latino High School Students: Evaluating the Segmented Assimilation Theory." *Sociological Perspectives* 52(2):159–183.

Katsouros, Stephen N. 2017. *Come to Believe: How the Jesuits Are Reinventing Education (Again)*. New York: Orbis Books.

Kearney, G. R. 2008. *More Than a Dream: How One School's Vision Is Changing the World*. Chicago: Loyola Press.

Keister, Lisa A. 2007. "Upward Wealth Mobility: Exploring the Roman Catholic Advantage." *Social Forces* 85(3):1195–1225.

Kelly, Andrew P., Jessica S. Howell, and Carolyn Sattin-Bajaj. 2016. "Introduction." In *Matching Students to Opportunity: Expanding College Choice, Access, and Quality*, 1–14. Cambridge, MA: Harvard Education Press.

Khan, Shamus Rahman. 2011. *Privilege: The Making of an Adolescent Elite at St. Paul's School*. Princeton, NJ: Princeton University Press.

Kim, Eunyoung, and Jeannette Díaz. 2013. "Immigrant Students and Higher Education." *ASHE: Higher Education Report* 38(6):1–169.

Kim, Hwan Doo, and Barbara Schneider. 2005. "Social Capital in Action: Alignment of Parental Support in Adolescents' Transition to Postsecondary Education." *Social Forces* 84(2):1181–1206.

Kim, Young K., and Linda J. Sax. 2009. "Student–Faculty Interaction in Research Universities: Differences by Student Gender, Race, Social Class, and First-Generation Status." *Research in Higher Education* 50(5):437–459.

Kiyama, Judy Ramos, and Cassandra Elena Harper. 2018. "Beyond Hovering: A Conceptual Argument for an Inclusive Model of Family Engagement in Higher Education." *Review of Higher Education* 41(3):365–385.

Kleinberg, S. J. 2006. *Widows and Orphans First: The Family Economy and Social Welfare Policy, 1880–1939.* Champaign: University of Illinois Press.

Klugman, Joshua. 2012. "How Resource Inequalities among High Schools Reproduce Class Advantages in College Destinations." *Research in Higher Education* 53:803–830.

Langenkamp, Amy G. 2011. "Effects of Educational Transitions on Students' Academic Trajectory: A Life Course Perspective." *Sociological Perspectives* 54(4):497–520.

Langenkamp, Amy G., and Andrew D. Hoyt. 2017. "Leaks in Latina/o Students' College-Going Pipeline: Consequences of Educational Expectation Attrition." *Journal of Hispanic Education.* December 25, 2017. https://doi.org/10.1177 /1538192717749878.

Lareau, Annette. 2011. *Unequal Childhoods: Race, Class, and Family Life. Second Edition. A Decade Later.* Berkeley: University of California Press.

———. 2015. "Cultural Knowledge and Social Inequality." *American Sociological Review* 80(1):1–27.

Lareau, Annette, Shani Aidia Evans, and April Yee. 2016. "The Rules of the Game and the Uncertain Transmission of Advantage: Middle-Class Parents' Search for an Urban Kindergarten." *Sociology of Education* 89(4):279–299.

Lawrence, Matthew. 2016. "Unequal Advantages: The Intergenerational Effects of Parental Educational Mobility." *American Education Research Journal* 53(1):71–99.

Lee, Elizabeth M. 2016. *Class and Campus Life: Managing and Experiencing Inequality at an Elite College.* Ithaca, NY: ILR Press.

Lee, Sang Min, Antoinette Thorn, Susana Contreras Bloomdahl, Jung Hee Ha, Suk Kyung Nam, and Jayoung Lee. 2012. "Parent Involvement in School: English Speaking versus Spanish Speaking Families." *Spanish Journal of Psychology* 15(2):582–591.

Lee, Stacey J. 2005. *Up Against Whiteness: Race, School, and Immigrant Youth.* New York: Teachers College Press.

Lehmann, Wolfgang. 2007. "'I Just Didn't Feel Like I Fit In': The Role of Habitus in University Drop-Out Decisions." *Canadian Journal of Higher Education* 37(2):89–110.

Lewis, Amanda E., and John B. Diamond. 2015. *Despite the Best Intentions: How Racial Inequality Thrives in Good Schools.* Oxford: Oxford University Press.

Lewis-McCoy, R. L'Heureux. 2014. *Inequality in the Promised Land: Race, Resources, and Suburban Schooling.* Stanford, CA: Stanford University Press.

Liebenthal, Ryan. 2018. "The Incredible, Rage-Inducing Inside Story of America's Student Debt Machine." *Mother Jones.* September/October 2018. www .motherjones.com/politics/2018/08/debt-student-loan-forgiveness-betsy-devos -education-department-fedloan.

Liu, Vivian Yuen Ting. 2016. "Do Students Benefit from Going Backward? The Academic and Labor Market Consequences of Four- to Two-Year College Transfer." Working paper, Community College Research Center, Teachers College, Columbia University. https://capseecenter.org/wp-content/uploads/2016 /06/capsee-do-students-benefit-from-going-backward.pdf.

London, Howard B. 1989. "Breaking Away: A Study of First-Generation College Students and Their Families." *American Journal of Education* 97:144–170.

———. 1992. "Transformations: Cultural Challenges Faced by First-Generation Students." *New Directions for Community Colleges* 80:5–11.

Loveday, Vik. 2016. "Embodying Deficiency through 'Affective Practice': Shame, Relationality, and the Lived Experience of Social Class and Gender in Higher Education." *Sociology* 50(6):1140–1155.

Lubrano, Alfred. 2005. *Limbo: Blue-Collar Roots, White-Collar Dreams*. New York: Wiley.

Marshall, Victor W., and Margaret M. Mueller. 2003. "Theoretical Roots of the Life-Course Perspective." In *Social Dynamics of the Life Course: Transitions, Institutions, and Interrelations*, edited by W. R. Heinz and V. W. Marshall, 3–32. New York: Aldine de Gruyter.

Martinez, Guadalupe F., and Regina Deil-Amen. 2015. "College for All Latinos? The Role of High School Messages in Facing College Challenges." *Teachers College Record* 117:1–50.

McCabe, Janice, and Brandon A. Jackson. 2016. "Pathways to Financing College: Race and Class in Students' Narratives of Paying for School." *Social Currents* 3(4):367–385.

McCloskey, Patrick J. 2011. *The Street Stops Here: A Year at a Catholic High School in Harlem*. Berkeley: University of California Press.

McDonough, Patricia M. 1997. *Choosing Colleges: How Social Class and Schools Structure Opportunity*. Albany: State University of New York Press.

McGuinness, Margaret M. 1995. "Body and Soul: Catholic Social Settlements and Immigration." *U.S. Catholic Historian* 13(3):63–75.

Meier, Deborah, and Emily Gasoi. 2017. *These Schools Belong to You and Me*. Boston: Beacon.

Merton, Robert K. 1987. "Three Fragments from a Sociologist's Notebooks: Establishing the Phenomenon, Specified Ignorance, and Strategic Research Materials." *Annual Review of Sociology* 13:1–28.

Mettler, Suzanne. 2014. *Degrees of Inequality: How the Politics of Higher Education Sabotaged the American Dream*. New York: Basic Books.

Miller, Ben. 2018. "Student Debt: It's Worse Than We Imagined." *New York Times*.

Miller-Adams, Michelle. 2015. "Promise Nation: Transforming Communities through Place-Based Scholarships." W.E. Upjohn Institute for Employment and Research.

Mullen, Ann. 2010. *Degrees of Inequality: Culture, Class, and Gender in American Higher Education*. Baltimore: Johns Hopkins University Press.

Nathan, Linda. 2017. *When Grit Isn't Enough: A High School Principal Examines How Poverty and Inequality Thwart the College-for-All Promise*. Boston: Beacon.

National Center for Education Statistics (NCES). 2017. Education Longitudinal Study (ELS 2002/2012). "Education Longitudinal Study of 2002." September 15, 2017. https://nces.ed.gov/surveys/els2002/.

———. 2018a. "The Condition of Education." https://nces.ed.gov/programs/coe/indicator_cgc.asp.

———. 2018b. "Median Annual Earnings of Full-Time Year-Round Workers Twenty-Five to Thirty-Four Years Old by Educational Attainment, 1995–2017 (in constant 2017 dollars). Table 502.30. September 10, 2018. https://nces.ed.gov/programs/digest/d18/tables/dt18_502.30.asp.

———. 2019. "Digest of Education Statistics." 53rd ed. January 30, 2019. https://nces.ed.gov/pubs2018/2018070.pdf.

National Council of Catholic Bishops (NCCB). 2000. "Welcoming the Stranger among Us: Unity in Diversity." National Council of Catholic Bishops, United States Catholic Conference. November 15, 2000.

National Student Clearinghouse (NSC). 2017. "Snapshot Report: Yearly Success and Progress Rates." March 13, 2017. https://nscresearchcenter.org/wp-content/uploads /SnapshotReport25.pdf.

Nativity Miguel Coalition (NMC). 2018. "Nativity Miguel Coalition: Breaking the Cycle of Poverty through Faith-Based Education." https://nativitymigueldotorg .wordpress.com.

Neal, D. 1997. "The Effects of Catholic Secondary Schooling on Educational Achievement." *Journal of Labor Economics* 15(1):98–123.

Nelson, Ingrid A. 2017. *Why Afterschool Matters.* New Brunswick, NJ: Rutgers University Press.

Newkirk, Thomas. 2017. *Embarrassment: And the Emotional Underlife of Learning.* Portsmouth, NH: Heinemann.

Ngai, Mae M. 2004. *Impossible Subjects: Illegal Aliens and the Making of Modern America.* Princeton, NJ: Princeton University Press.

Nichols, Laura. 2014. "Social Desire Paths: A New Theoretical Concept to Increase the Usability of Social Science Research in Society." *Theory and Society* 43(6):647–665.

———. 2017. "The Role of Catholic Schools in Reducing Educational and Economic Inequality." *Integritas* 9(4):1–25.

———.2019 (forthcoming). "Addressing Exclusion in Organizations: Social Desire Paths and Undocumented Students Attending College." *Social Problems.*

Nichols, Laura, and Maria Guzmán. 2017. "Getting, Staying, and Being in College: The Experiences of Students." In *Undocumented and in College: Students and Institutions in a Climate of National Hostility,* edited by Terry-Ann Jones and Laura Nichols, 104–133. New York: Fordham University Press.

Nichols Laura, and Ángel Islas. 2016. "Pushing and Pulling Emerging Adults through College: College Generational Status and the Influence of Parents and Others in the First Year." *Journal of Adolescent Research* 31(1):59–95.

Noll, Elizabeth, Lindsey Reichlin, and Barbara Gault. 2017. "College Students with Children: National and Regional Profiles." IWPR 451. Washington, DC: Institute for Women's Policy Research. https://iwpr.org/publications/college-students -children-national-regional-profiles/.

Nora, Amaury, and Alberto F. Cabrera 1996. "The Role of Perceptions of Prejudice and Discrimination on the Adjustment of Minority Students to College." *Journal of Higher Education* 67(2):119–148.

Nunn, Lisa M. 2014. *Defining Student Success: The Role of School and Culture.* New Brunswick, NJ: Rutgers University Press.

———. 2018. *33 Simple Strategies for Faculty: A Week-by-Week Resource for Teaching First-Year and First-Generation Students.* New Brunswick, NJ: Rutgers University Press.

Ochoa, Gilda L. 2013. *Academic Profiling: Latinos, Asian Americans, and the Achievement Gap.* Minneapolis: University of Minnesota Press.

Offer, Shira, and Barbara Schneider. 2007. "Children's Role in Generating Social Capital." *Social Forces* 85(3):1125–1142.

Orellana, Majorie Faulstich. 2003. "Responsibilities of Children in Latino Immigrant Homes." *New Directions for Youth Development* 100:25–39.

———. 2009. *Translating Childhoods: Immigrant Youth, Language, and Culture.* Rutgers, NJ: Rutgers University Press.

Ospino, Hosffman, and Patricia Weitzel-O'Neill. 2016. "Catholic Schools in an Increasingly Hispanic Church. A Summary Report of Findings from the National

Survey of Catholic Schools Serving Hispanic Families." Roche Center for Catholic Education, Boston College.

Ovink, Sarah M. 2017. *Race, Class, and Choice in Latino/a Higher Education: Pathways in the College-for-All Era.* New York: Palgrave Macmillan.

Ovink, Sarah, Demetra Kalogrides, Megan Nanney, and Patrick Delaney. 2018. "College Match and Undermatch: Assessing Student Preferences, College Proximity, and Inequality in Post-College Outcomes." *Research in Higher Education* 59:553–590.

Owens, Ann. 2010. "Neighborhoods and Schools as Competing and Reinforcing Contexts for Educational Attainment." *Sociology of Education* 83(4):287–311.

Paat, Yok-Fong. 2013. "Working with Immigrant Children and Their Families: An Application of Bronfenbrenner's Ecological Systems Theory." *Journal of Human Behavior in the Social Environment* 23:954–966.

Pascarella, Ernest T., Christopher T. Pierson, Gregory C. Wolniak, and Patrick T. Terenzini. 2004. "First-Generation College Students: Additional Evidence on College Experiences and Outcomes." *Journal of Higher Education* 75(3):249–284.

Pascarella, Ernest T., Gregory C. Wolniak, Christopher T. Pierson, and Patrick T. Terenzini. 2003. "Experiences and Outcomes of First-Generation Students in Community Colleges." *Journal of College Student Development* 44(4):420–429.

Pérez, Patricia A., and Patricia M. McDonough. 2008. "Understanding Latina and Latino College Choice: A Social Capital and Chain Migration Analysis." *Journal of Hispanic Higher Education* 7(3):249–265.

Perna, Laura W. 2002. "Precollege Outreach Programs: Characteristics of Programs Serving Historically Underrepresented Groups of Students." *Journal of College Student Development* 43(1):64–83.

Perna, Laura W., Michelle Asha Cooper, and Chunyan Li. 2010. "Conclusions and Recommendations for Policy, Practice, and Future Research." In *Understanding the Working College Student,* edited by Laura W. Perna, 283–307. Sterling: Stylus Publishing.

Pew Research Center. 2014. "The Religious Landscape, California." www.pewforum .org/religious-landscape-study/state/california/religious-tradition/catholic/.

———. 2016. "5 Facts about Latinos and Education."July 28, 2016. www.pewresearch.org /fact-tank/2016/07/28/5-facts-about-latinos-and-education/ft_16-07-26_latinoseduca-tion_collegecompletion/.

Pike, Gary R., and George D. Kuh. 2005. "First- and Second-Generation College Students: A Comparison of Their Engagement and Intellectual Development." *Journal of Higher Education* 76(3):276–300.

Pitre, Charisse Cowan, and Paul Pitre. 2009. "Increasing Underrepresented High School Students' College Transitions and Achievements: TRIO Educational Opportunity Programs." *NASSP Bulletin* 93(2):96–110.

Portes, Alejandro, and Rubén G. Rumbaut. 2006. *Immigrant America.* Berkeley: University of California Press.

Public Policy Institute of California (PPIC). 2018. "Higher Education: California Is Facing a Shortfall of College-Educated Workers." Public Policy Institute of California. January 2018.

Ramakrishnan, S. Karthick, and Hans P. Johnson. 2005. "Second-Generation Immigrants in California." www.ppic.org/content/pubs/cacounts/CC_505KRCC.pdf.

Redford, Jeremy, and Kathleen Mulvaney Hoyer. 2017. "First-Generation and Continuing-Generation College Students: A Comparison of High School and

Postsecondary Experiences." Stats in Brief. NCES 2018-009. U.S. Department of Education. September 2017.

Rivas-Drake, Deborah, and Margarita Mooney. 2008. "Profiles of Latino Adaptation at Elite Colleges and Universities." *American Journal of Community Psychology* 42(1–2):1–16.

Roderick, Melissa, Vanessa Coca, and Jenny Nagaoka. 2011. "Potholes on the Road to College: High School Effects in Shaping Urban Students' Participation in College Application, Four-Year College Enrollment, and College Match." *Sociology of Education* 84(3):178–211.

Rondini, Ashley C., Bedelia Nicola Richards, and Nicolas P. Simon. 2018. *Clearing the Path for First-Generation College Students: Qualitative and Intersectional Studies of Educational Mobility.* New York: Lexington Books.

Ryken, Amy E. 2006. "Multiple Choices, Multiple Chances: Fostering Re-entry Pathways for First Generation College Students." *Community College Journal of Research and Practice* 30:593–607.

Saenz, Victor B., Sylvia Hurtado, Doug Barrera, De'Sha Wolf, and Fanny Yeung. 2007. "First in My Family: A Profile of First-Generation College Students at Four-Year Institutions since 1971." Higher Education Research Institute. https://heri.ucla.edu/PDFs/resSummary051807-FirstGen.pdf.

Sallie Mae. 2018. "2017 How America Pays for College." https://news.salliemae.com/sites/salliemae.newshq.businesswire.com/files/doc_library/file/How_America_Pays_for_College_2017_Report.pdf.

Sampson, Robert J. 2012. *Chicago and the Enduring Neighborhood Effect.* Chicago: University of Chicago Press.

Schlossberg, Nancy K., Elinor B. Waters, and Jane Goodman. 1995. *Counseling Adults in Transition: Linking Practice with Theory.* 2nd ed. New York: Springer.

Schwadel, Philip, John D. McCarthy, and Hart M. Nelsen. 2009. "The Continuing Relevance of Family Income for Religious Participation: U.S. White Catholic Church Attendance in the Late 20th Century." *Social Forces* 87(4):1997–2030.

Selee, Andrew D. 2018. *Vanishing Frontiers: The Forces Driving Mexico and the United States Together.* New York: Public Affairs.

Sennett, Richard, and Jonathan Cobb. 1973. *The Hidden Injuries of Class.* New York: Vintage Books.

Settersten, Richard A., Jr. 2005. "Social Policy and the Transition to Adulthood." In *On the Frontier of Adulthood: Theory, Research, and Public Policy,* edited by R. A. Settersten, F. F. Furstenberg, and R. G. Rumbaut, 534–560. Chicago: University of Chicago Press.

———. 2011. "Becoming an Adult: Meanings and Markers for Young Americans." In *Coming of Age in America: The Transition to Adulthood in the Twenty-First Century,* edited by Mary C. Waters, Patrick Joseph Carr, Maria Kefalas, and Jennifer Ann Holdaway, 169–190. Berkeley: University of California Press.

Shalaby, Carla. 2017. *Troublemakers: Lessons in Freedom from Young Children at School.* New York: New Press.

Shumaker, Ryan, and Luke J. Wood. 2016. "Understanding First-Generation Community College Students: An Analysis of Covariance Examining Use of, Access to, and Efficacy Regarding Institutionally Offered Services." *Community College Enterprise* 22(2):9–17.

Silver, Alexis. 2018. *Shifting Boundaries: Immigrant Youth Negotiating National, State, and Small-Town Politics.* Stanford, CA: Stanford University Press.

Smart, Christopher. 2018. "New National Study: Immigrants in Sanctuary Cities Cooperate More Fully with Police, Moderating Crime and Making Communities Safer." *Salt Lake Tribune.* January 2018. www.sltrib.com/news/2018/01/08/fearful -of-deportation-unauthorized-immigrants-in-salt-lake-city-are-not-reporting-crime -police-chief-says/.

Stephen, Lynn. 2007. *Transborder Lives: Indigenous Oaxacans in Mexico, California, and Oregon.* Durham, NC: Duke University Press.

Stuber, Jenny M. 2011. *Inside the College Gates: How Class and Culture Matter in Higher Education.* Boulder, CO: Lexington Books.

Swail, Watson Scott. 2000. "Preparing America's Disadvantaged for College: Programs that Increase College Opportunity." *New Directions for Institutional Research* 107:85–101.

Swail, Watson Scott and Laura W. Perna. 2002. "Pre-College Outreach Programs: A National Perspective." In *Increasing Access to College: Extending Possibilities for All Students,* edited by W. G. Tierney and L. S. Hagedorn, 15–34. New York: Suny Press.

Swecker, Hadyn K., Matthew Fifolt, and Linda Searby. 2013. "Academic Advising and First-Generation College Students: A Quantitative Study on Student Retention." *NACADA Journal* 33(1):46–53.

Sy, Susan R. 2006. "Family and Work Influences on the Transition to College among Latina Adolescents." *Hispanic Journal of Behavioral Sciences* 28(3):368–386.

Taylor, Paul. 2014. *The Next America: Boomers, Millennials, and the Looming Generational Showdown.* New York: Public Affairs.

Terenzini, Patrick T., Leonard Springer, Patricia M. Yaeger, Ernest T. Pascarella, and Amaury Nora. 1996. "First-Generation College Students: Characteristics, Experiences, and Cognitive Development." *AIR Forum Issue* 37(1):1–22.

Thelin, John R. 2004. *A History of American Higher Education.* Baltimore: Johns Hopkins University Press.

Torres, Kimberly, and Douglas S. Massey. 2012. "Fitting In: Segregation, Social Class, and the Experiences of Black Students at Selective Colleges and Universities." *Race and Social Problems* 4:171–192.

Turley, Ruth N. López. 2009. "College Proximity: Mapping Access to Opportunity." *Sociology of Education* 82:126–146.

Turley, Ruth N. López, Martín Santos, and Cecilia Ceja. 2007. "Social Origin and College Opportunity Expectations across Cohorts." *Social Science Research* 36(3):1200–1218.

U.S. Census Bureau. 2018. "CPS Historical Time Series Tables, Years of School Completed by People 25 Years and Over, Selected Years 1940–2017." August 15, 2018. https://www.census.gov/data/tables/time-series/demo/educational-attainment/cps -historical-time-series.html.

Valentine, Jeffrey C., Amy S. Hirschy, Christine D. Bremer, Walter Novillo, Marisa Castellano, and Aaron Banister. 2011. "Keeping At-Risk Students in School: A Systematic Review of College Retention Programs." *Educational Evaluation and Policy Analysis* 33(2):214–234.

Vallejo, Jody Agius. 2012. *Barrios to Burbs: The Making of the Mexican American Middle Class.* Stanford, CA: Stanford University Press.

Velez, Erin Dunlop, Alexander Bentz, and Caren Arbeit. 2018. "Working before, during, and after Beginning at a Public 2-Year Institution: Labor Market Experiences of

Community College Students." Stats in Brief 2018-428. National Center for Education Statistics.

Vuong, Mui, Sharon Brown-Welty, and Susan Tracz. 2010. "The Effects of Self-Efficacy on Academic Success of First-Generation College Sophomore Students." *Journal of College Student Development* 51(1):50–64.

Waldinger, Roger, and Renee Reichl. 2006. "Second-Generation Mexicans: Getting Ahead or Falling Behind?" Migration Policy Institute. www.migrationpolicy.org /article/second-generation-mexicans-getting-ahead-or-falling-behind/.

Walpole, MaryBeth. 2003. "Socioeconomic Status and College: How SES Affects College Experiences and Outcomes." *Review of Higher Education* 27(1):45–73.

———. 2007. "Economically and Educationally Challenged Students in Higher Education: Access to Outcomes." *ASHE Higher Education Report* 33(3):1–113.

Ward, Janie Victoria. 2000. *The Skin We're In: Teaching Our Children to Be Emotionally Strong, Socially Smart, and Spiritually Connected*. New York: Free Press.

———. 2018. "Lessons in Resistance and Resilience." *Diversity & Democracy* 21(1):13–15.

Wartman, Katherine Lynk, and Marjorie Savage. 2008. "Parental Involvement in Higher Education: Understanding the Relationship among Students, Parents, and the Institution." *ASHE Higher Education Report* 33(6):1–125.

Waters, Mary C., Patrick Joseph Carr, Maria Kefalas, and Jennifer Ann Holdaway, eds. 2010. *Coming of Age in America: The Transition to Adulthood in the Twenty-First Century*. Berkeley: University of California Press.

Waters, Mary C., and Marisa Gerstein Pineau. 2015. *Integration of Immigrants into American Society*. Silver Spring, MD: Committee on Catholic Legal Immigration Network.

Weisskirch, Robert S., ed. 2017. *Language Brokering in Immigrant Families: Theories and Contexts*. New York: Routledge.

Wimer, Christopher, Marybeth Mattingly, Sara Kimberlin, Jonathan Fisher, Caroline Danielson, and Sarah Bohn. 2018. "2.1 Million Californians in Deep Poverty." July 2018. https://inequality.stanford.edu/sites/default/files/california_poverty_measure_2016.pdf.

Wirth, Eileen. 2007. *They Made All the Difference: Life-Changing Stories from Jesuit High Schools*. Chicago: Loyola Press.

Yoo, Grace J., and Barbara W. Kim. 2014. *Caring across Generations: The Linked Lives of Korean American Families*. New York: New York University Press.

Zhou, Min. 2001. "Progress, Decline, Stagnation? The New Second Generation Comes of Age." In *Strangers at the Gates: New Immigrants in Urban America*, edited by R. Waldinger, 272–307. Berkeley: University of California Press.

Zhou, Min, and Jennifer Lee. 2007. "Becoming Ethnic or Becoming American? Reflecting on the Divergent Pathways to Social Mobility and Assimilation among the New Second Generation." *Du Bois Review* 4(1):189–205.

Zinshteyn, Mikhail. 2018. "California Lacks System to Track Students through High School, College, and Workplace." EdSource. May 17, 2018. www.edsource.org.

Ziskin, Mary, Vasti Torres, Don Hossler, and Jacob P. K. Gross. 2010. "Mobile Working Students: A Delicate Balance of College, Family, and Work." In *Understanding the Working College Student*, edited by Laura W. Perna, 67–92. Sterling: Stylus Publishing.

Index

About the Author

LAURA NICHOLS is an associate professor of sociology at Santa Clara University in California, where she teaches and conducts community-based research. She co-edited, with Terry-Ann Jones, *Undocumented and in College: Students and Institutions in a Climate of National Hostility*.